Gift of
Miss Agnes Clements
Christmas 1963

NEW HORIZONS

NEW HORIZONS

Studies in Biblical Theology

by Barnabas M. Ahern, C.P.

Edited by Carroll Stuhlmueller, C.P.

With a foreword by

Mother Kathryn Sullivan, R.S.C.J.

FIDES PUBLISHERS, INC.

NOTRE DAME, INDIANA

To

Most Reverend Malcolm La Velle, C.P.
Superior General

and

Reverend Boniface Fielding, C.P.
Former Provincial

Their interest in scriptural studies
prepared the way for this book.

ACKNOWLEDGMENTS

Permission to reprint material in this book is gratefully acknowledged from the following publishers and periodicals: Chapter 1, *The Critic* (August-September, 1962); chapter 2, Herder and Herder, publishers of *The Bridge* for the Institute of Judaeo-Christian Studies, Seton Hall University, Newark, N. J. (chapter 2 appeared in volume one of *The Bridge,* 1955); chapter 3, *Cross and Crown,* September, 1959; chapter 4, *Chicago Studies,* Spring, 1962; chapter 5, a transcript, slightly revised, of a taped lecture delivered at the Passionist Seminary Congress held at Mother of Good Counsel Seminary, Warrenton, Missouri, 1962; chapter 6, revised version of article from *Catholic Biblical Quarterly,* January, 1960; chapter 7, *Student World,* No. 1, 1962; chapter 8, Catholic Theological Society of America (Proceedings, 1961); chapter 9, Catholic College Teachers of Sacred Doctrine (Proceedings, 1961); chapter 10, The Liturgical Conference (Proceedings, National Liturgical Week, 1954); chapter 11, *Perspectives,* September-October, 1962.

FOREWORD

I T WAS a happy thought to assemble some of the numerous
and widely scattered articles written by Father Barnabas
M. Ahern, C.P. so as to enrich both those for whom
these pages are a memory and those for whom they are a
discovery. Written at different times and in many places
they possess unity and obvious diversity. However varied
the themes may be, theirs is the inner unity that comes from
identity of form and purpose. The entire approach is that
of biblical theology. The single goal is "Christ in his fulness."

Much of present day interest in Scripture can be traced
to the invitation offered scholars by Pius XII in his encyclical *Divino afflante Spiritu.* There he urged that the theological riches of every biblical book and every significant
text be explored, so that the study of revelation in the light
of human reason might bring the courage that comes of
new-found joy and the strength that is born of deeper insight
into truth. The word of the exegete about the word of God
is not meant to be a sterile speculation but an illumination

enabling souls to reach what modern writers have called "the still point" where time and eternity meet, or "the moment of truth" where the mystery of life is seen in unsuspected beauty and death is found to be completion not privation, or "the moment of reality" when we understand as never before that "love is the meaning" of every heartache, brief pleasure and hard won knowledge.

The Protagoras is one of Plato's most deft and amusing dialogues. Its main subject can be summed up in two questions: What is virtue? Can it be taught? To read these pages of Athenian wit is to delight in their brilliance, to be impressed by their underlying gravity and to see how far and how far short human answers go.

To ask the same questions in a biblical context is to become involved in the story of God's love for man, as we find it recorded in Sacred Scripture. This is the story of salvation, the *Heilsgeschichte,* the sequence of divine interventions which shape history from creation to the parousia, from the Old Testament to the New Testament, from the New Testament to the Church. It is within this frame of reference that the chapters of this book have an important place.

The Old Testament background of the first chapters shows that the thoughts, hopes, ideals and sorrows of God's people combined not only to sanctify them but also to provide a portrait of the Promised One. The New Testament background of the later chapters shows that when Christ came, He so thoroughly united Himself with all men, that only with them and through them can He be fully known. The heart of the book therefore can be described in Pauline terms as a study of the "body" of Christ, the whole Christ with all His members. This body is already glorified because its life is that of the risen Christ. Day by day in the

Church His glory is transforming the "body" of Christ into "Christ." The Christian answer to the questions that vexed Plato and his friends becomes luminously plain.

To miss this answer is for a Christian the only failure in life that matters. Even Plato's disciples understood the importance of the vision of truth. Plotinus, the last of the great philosophers of the ancient world and their heir, could discount all other failures provided man attain true understanding.

> "For not he who has failed of the joy that is in color or visible forms, not he who has failed of power or of honors or of kingdoms has failed; but he who has failed of this alone, for whose winning he should renounce kingdoms and the rule of earth and sea and sky, if only spurning beneath his feet the world of sense, and straining forward to this, he may see."

To this vision, of which the Pauline equivalent is a deeper awareness of "the fulness of Christ," these chapters can lead. Awareness alone, however, is not enough. Vision should lead to action. Jesus, the Word of the Father, could say to His disciples: "As the Father hath sent me, I also send you." This divinely shared mission makes those whom He has chosen, like Himself, a living word, that is, a continuing revelation of infinite mercy and love. This message is both new and old. It is old because it goes back to the beginning when the Word was with God and when through that Word all things were made. It is new because each disciple receives this message according to the measure of his own generosity and carries it to a world whose horizons are limited only by his zeal.

There are thinkers today who place their readers in an either/or situation, asking them to choose between a man-centered or a cosmos-centered world. Father Barnabas offers no such false confrontation. Of this the title of his book is both guarantee and guide. Moving into another dimension, he asks us to consider man and his world in the true perspective of divine light. These new horizons do not force us to choose between earth and heaven but show that heaven and earth form part of a greater whole. Understanding such as this leads to dialogue.

Thought is the dialogue of the soul with itself. Prayer is the dialogue of the soul with God. This book will help both forms of communication and make possible a third form in which soul meets souls and God. This is another way of describing the biblical vision of Christian life, a view that is all ardor and sacrifice and self-forgetful love.

The message of this book is meant for every *interested* Christian. Learned footnotes and technical explanations have been omitted lest those with little Hebrew and scant Greek be turned away from so much good. Those with a flair for the scholarly and a training for the scientific are urged to consult the original sources of these articles in the list provided by Father Carroll Stuhlmueller, C.P., the painstaking and generous editor of this book, who has placed all its readers in his debt.

MOTHER KATHRYN SULLIVAN, R.S.C.J.
Manhattanville College of the Sacred Heart
Purchase, New York

CONTENTS

CHAPTER 1 NEW HORIZONS

THE year 1943 marked a turning point in Catholic Scripture studies. With the publication of the encyclical *Divino afflante Spiritu,* Pope Pius XII voiced official approval of a distinctively modern approach to the Bible. While insuring the permanence of the Church's age-old understanding of God's word, he also opened wide the door to all the gains which modern scholarship could achieve.

This papal letter was the outgrowth of long development both outside and within the Catholic church. From the year 1850 scholars had been tracing an odyssey which discovered new fields, led to new heights, and often lost itself in devious bypaths. The vicissitudes of the way which scientific scholarship has followed are now familiar to us all; Jean Levie has rehearsed the story in his book, *The Bible, Word of God in Words of Men* (Kenedy, 1961). Pope Pius approved all that was true in the course which science had pursued, canonized it as a necessary way for all Scripture scholarship to follow, and urged Catholic students of the Bible to labor for "the happy and fruitful union between the doctrine and spiritual sweetness of expression of the ancient authors and the greater erudition and maturer knowledge of the modern."

It is time now to assess the cardinal elements of the modern scriptural advance and to see how these provide new perspectives and unfold new horizons for Christian living.

The contemporary Scripture movement began with the discovery of the world of the Bible. Excavation at biblical sites, the discovery of whole libraries of Near Eastern literature, the deciphering of ancient languages and law codes— all this opened the Bible wide to light which revealed meanings hitherto unknown. Students of the Scriptures came to realize that Israel and Christianity were not born in a vacuum. Events and personalities, social practices and ethical mores recorded in the Bible are rooted in the soil of the ancient Near East. Men and women of the biblical period were children of their own age and culture; their thought patterns and images were colored with the tints of Semitic surroundings; their very language followed the rhythm of Semitic parallelism.

This awareness that God's work took shape and color from the ancient world of the Near East is of fundamental importance in modern Scripture studies. Though God loves "all things that are" (Wisd. 11:24) and can put an "At Home" sign on the door of any people, He deliberately chose the descendants of Abraham to be witnesses and recipients of His wonders. To understand His work, therefore, we must know the life and culture of this nation to whom He said, "You shall be my special possession, dearer to me than all other people" (Ex. 19:5).

Skim through the Book of Genesis. The account of the first man and woman is presented in the Semitic thought-patterns of the Babylonian hymn, *Enuma Elish*. The Deluge narrative of Genesis 6ff. is similar to many other flood stories circulating in the Near East and bears striking resemblance, especially, to the Gilgamesh epic. The history of Abraham is woven warp and woof of the social practices and cultural life of the wandering Amorrhites who spread across the Fertile Crescent from Babylon to Chanaan in the early second millenium before Christ. The enigmatic story of Abraham's sacrifice of Isaac is understandable only as a preventive against the practice of slaughtering the first-born, the cruel Chanaanite ritual to appease the gods and win their blessing for a large progeny.

The story of Sodom and Gomorra is merely a unique treatment of one instance of widespread Chanaanite perversion. The patriarchs' multiplication of wives and their cavalier way of dealing with less favored members of their harems represent life just as it was being lived and as it was legislated for in the contemporary codes of Hammurabi and in the regulatory laws recently discovered at Nuzi and Mari. Social practices which so offend our sensibilities become meaningful when we see them in the light of a patriarchal social structure in which the tribe with its father-sheik was the unit of society rather than the individual family, as with us.

God simply accepted men as He found them and quietly worked out His purpose within the limitations of a civilization in which conscience would develop only through the persistent influence of His revelation.

The whole course of Israel's history and the emergence of its highest ideals are rightly understood only within the context of the nation's life. Its shocking practices in war are exactly the same as the cruel exploits of the neighboring nations which are described for us in the Mesa stone discovered just east of the Dead Sea by Clermont-Ganneau in 1868. Israel's bid for kingship seems to have been prompted by envy of the newly created Aramean states on the other side of the Jordan. The importance of the Queen-Mother in the kingdom of Juda parallels perfectly the status of the *gebirah* in the Hittite kingdom of Boghaz-koi.

The land of Palestine, torn by war, honeycombed with vice and corruption, consecrated by the true worship of God, is the stage on which Israel's prophets proclaimed their divine message. Were it not for the backdrop of life in Israel, the voice of the prophets would have melted into thin air. Their message of God's personal concern and moral demands gained resonance by echoing within the framework of their own times. Rarely did they direct their categorical imperatives to the universe; the primary function of these preachers was to act as mentors of Israel. The moral conscience of the nation was progressively enlightened as its devious course was perennially straightened by the stern rebukes of God's spokesmen.

The daily life of the nation provided the soil for the seed of hope to grow and for the word of God to mature into dogma. From the very beginning Israel was a forward-looking people. God's word had promised a wonderful future which always seemed just around the corner. The accession of each new king to the throne of David seemed to be the moment for the breakthrough of God's salvation. Each king, therefore, was greeted as the favored son of God who would bring all good things to God's nation:

> May he endure as long as the sun,
>   and like the moon through all generations . . . .
> Justice shall flower in his days,
>   and profound peace, till the moon be no more
> May he rule from sea to sea,
>   and from the River to the ends of the earth.
>   (Ps. 71:5, 7, 8)

One after another, however, the kings of Israel failed to realize this fervent dream. God's promise, nevertheless, could not fail. Naturally, therefore, Israel began to look forward to an ideal king of the future through whom God would accomplish all His promised works. Thus kingship itself became an agent in the development of the nation's messianic expectancy.

It was the same with the dogmas of Israel. Their development required not only the seed of God's revealing word but the soil of the nation's life. This is clearly seen in the development of the doctrine of retribution. In the beginning a blessed after-life was incomprehensible to men who thought always in terms of an animated and personalized body. Whatever reward man received had to be something physical and earthly. When such rewards failed to materialize, Israel began to hope for the fulfillment of God's promise in life after death. Eventual contact with the Greek mind in Egypt brought new awareness of man's spiritual power to experience joy and sorrow even apart from the body. The soil of Jewish thought was thus prepared for the sublime doctrine of retribution presented in the Greek Book of Wisdom.

In the New Testament it is quite the same. God works in humanness; seed and soil are both necessary for the harvest. Modern students of the Bible are probing beneath the word of the Gospel to discover the exact limits and proportions of Jesus' self-revelation. As a Jew speaking to Jews He not only used their language and employed their imagery, but also accepted their thought-patterns as the vehicle for manifesting Himself and declaring His mission.

Because the Jews were looking forward to a new Israel, the beneficiary of wonders even greater than those which their ancestors had received, Jesus identified Himself as the new Israel in His baptism, in His temptations, and in the new law which, like another Moses, He charted for the guidance of those who would become true Israelites. The fullness of His mission found perfect description in concepts which Israel itself had forged. Isaia's portrait of the Servant of Yahweh and Daniel's glorification of the Son of Man provided Him with models for self-identification and for the prosecution of His messianic vocation.

His method of teaching followed the pattern used by the rabbis of His own day. Many of His words show the coloring both of Old Testament language and of the rabbinical discourse of His own time. Recent discoveries at Qumran indicate that the language of Jesus in the fourth Gospel, previously so difficult to explain, bears remarkable resemblance to much of the terminology and to many of the thought-patterns of the Qumran community. As Père Leonce de Grandmaison has beautifully expressed it, God's transcendent truths are reflected in the human language and deeds of Christ like sunlight shining on a limpid pool. For Him the divine found perfect mirroring in the human.

This interplay of the divine and human is always to the fore in the letters of Paul. There is no question that his doctrine underwent development. The strongly eschatological concern of his epistles to the Thessalonians, his first, eventually changes into the theme of realized eschatology in Colossians and Ephesians. His early emphasis on Christ's resurrection eventually enlarges to include also His redemptive death. His first mention of "life in Christ" grows into the complete teaching of his later epistles with their full doctrine on Christ as head and Christians as members of His body.

Many of these developments owed their origin to an immediate challenge in the life of the community. The needs of his converts and the controversies which he had to wage were for Paul the anvil on which he beat out the sparks of his illuminating doctrine. His mind and understanding grew through application of the mystery of Jesus to the pressing needs of the here and now.

The conclusion of all this for modern biblical scholarship is obvious. If an exegete is to measure God's revelatory action accurately he must be thoroughly familiar with the imagery and though-patterns, with the ways of life and modes of culture in which the word of God incarnated itself. He can gauge exactly the divine manifestation only when he has come alive to the tone and color of the human event in which God's word took flesh. Pius XII gave classic expression to this imperative demand of modern study of the Bible. He wrote: "Let the interpreter, then, with all care and without neglecting any light derived from recent research, endeavor to determine the peculiar character and circumstances of the sacred writer, the age in which he lived, the sources written or oral to which he had recourse and the forms of expression he employed."

Equal in importance to the thesis of biblical origins in human surroundings is the corresponding thesis of biblical origins in human recountal. Scholars today have come to realize that a marked social quality characterizes the human agency which functioned in the preparation of the sacred books. Whereas inspiration was formerly thought of as a grace which touched the mind and will of a unique and self-sufficient literary author, today this action of God is seen to have influenced many human elements in a group contribution to the formation of biblical literature. Karl Rahner, beyond all others, has pressed this claim. For him a book is inspired insofar as it represents authentically the doctrine and insights of the apostolic Church. To be an inspired book a literary work must be a Church book.

This emphasis on the social quality of inspiration flows

logically from widely accepted principles on how the Bible came into being. At the turn of the century Hermann Gunkel pointed out that the Book of Genesis shows marked similarity to other forms of literature which originated orally. Whereas earlier scholars had explained Genesis as an amalgam of previously written documents, the Yahwist, Elohist, Deuteronomist and Priestly sources, Gunkel preferred to emphasize the more important factor of oral tradition. In sacred recitals at the sanctuaries and in folk songs around the campfire, Israel shaped and preserved the materials which form our Old Testament.

What Gunkel began, the Swedish school of Uppsala brought to further perfection. Not only Genesis but the greater part of the Old Testament represents a celebration of the deeds of God in the sacred memorial rites of God's people. In its shrine centers at Bethel and Dan, Hebron and Jerusalem, Israel heartened itself with new courage by recalling in song and saga the wonderful interventions of God throughout the long course of its history. Everything was grist for its mill. Popular stories and legends, divine miracles and brave deeds of yore, great national upheavals and personal exploits of local heroes—all these elements were recalled with grateful memory and were constantly transformed with an ever developing insight into the profound purposes of God and with growing awareness of His guiding providence.

Men of ardent faith had prophetic vision to see in the events of the past a history which God Himself had created. History recounted in this spirit was bound to nourish faith. To borrow words from St. Paul, "In it the justice of God is revealed, from faith unto faith" (Rom. 1:17). Through such memories men became vitally aware that God was always a saving God, in the present as much as in the past.

They began to understand more clearly the full import of the name which He had chosen for Himself, *Yahweh,* "He who is." He is the God who is always there, always at hand to deliver and to save, just as once long ago He had rescued His people from the tyranny of Egypt and bound them fast to Himself in the covenant of Sinai.

For Israel, therefore, sacred history was something more than a bare recountal of colorless deeds of the past. It was rather an awesome manifestation of divine power and glory which is always at work "yesterday, today, yes, and forever" (Heb. 13:8). Israel saw its past in the light of an ardent faith which revealed in the history of men the saving deeds of God.

Such history was existential in the fullest sense of the word, dynamically relevant to the here and now. Listening to this story devout worshippers came alive with new awareness of what God wanted to do in their own lives. The recountal of the Exodus did something more than inspire grateful memories of the past; it rang a challenge to fidelity in the present. That is why the story ends with the reminder, "not with our fathers did he make this covenant, but with us, all of us, who are alive here this day" (Deut. 5:2-3).

Memories of this kind gave fresh confidence in the present help of Yahweh. Listening to what God had done for their ancestors, the Israelites of Michea's day cried out. "As in the days when you came from the land of Egypt, show us wonderful signs" (Mic. 7:15). To hear what God had done meant instant response in the here and now. This explains why the liturgical recountal of His deeds often ended with the pointed reminder, "That today you would hear his voice: 'Harden not your hearts'" (Ps. 94:7f).

Again, all this is true of the New Testament. For too

long a time we have regarded the Gospels as a biography of Christ prepared by the careful historians, Matthew, Mark, Luke and John. It required the labors of non-Catholic liberal scholars to remind us of a thesis which Catholics should never have forgotten. We have always insisted that thirty years of oral preaching preceded the composition of the written Gospels. It was the German school of form-criticism which forced us to face the implications of a position which Catholic tradition has always treasured.

At the end of the First World War these German scholars began applying the principles of Hermann Gunkel to the New Testament. Men like Rudolf Bultmann and Martin Dibelius, Karl Schmidt and Bertram Schweizer looked upon the Gospels as the creation of the primitive Christian community and analyzed the form of each successive unit to discover the sociological factor which brought it into being. Preaching and instruction, controversy and liturgy—these were the factors which led the community to prepare in oral form the "miracle stories" and logia, the "pronouncement stories" and liturgical recountals which eventually found place in the written Gospels.

It is true that we cannot accept the basic philosophic postulates of the early form-critics, who were dominated by Heidegger's philosophy. To ascribe creativity to an anonymous community, as they did, is both philosophically and theologically unsound. At the same time, however, Catholic exegetes are happy to benefit from the emphasis which these scholars have placed on the formative action of oral tradition in the transmission of the words and deeds of Jesus.

We know now that events are recorded in the Gospels not merely because Jesus performed them but, above all, because the early Christian community cherished them as directives for Church life and guide-lines for personal conduct. Every unit of the Gospel shows the mark of community use. Miracles are related not as documentary accounts of the deeds of Christ but as terse action photos of the messianic mercy which He is always ready to renew. The Last Supper is recounted in the synoptics not as a photographic reproduction of all that took place but as a sacramental rite which is constantly being renewed in the "breaking of bread." Some of our Lord's most telling pronouncements are preserved in the Gospel not because they were intended for the use of future biographers but because they were used every day in the life of the community to meet the challenge of its foes and to form Christlike attitudes in men and women who, though followers of Christ, had never seen Him.

Like the history of Israel, the history of Jesus is a saving history. For thirty years before the composition of the first Gospel, the events of His life were told and re-told with sublime faith in their present efficacy. The works of His human life mark the culmination of God's saving action in the world of men. Like all sacred history, therefore, they are dynamically relevant in every age: "Jesus Christ is the same, yesterday and today, yes, and forever" (Heb. 13:8).

No writer has made such capital of biblical teaching as did the Apostle Paul. He who is looked upon as a rugged individualist and the creative artist of the Church's theology is in reality the most traditional of thinkers. True, he rarely cites historical details in the life of Jesus and hardly ever quotes His words. Unlike the author of the Epistle to the Hebrews, he does not delay over lengthy expositions of passages from the Old Testament. He is too much concerned with the present relevance of God's work to spend his words on exact historical reproduction. Paul thoroughly familiar with all of Scripture, weaves its motifs into a finished masterpiece which orchestrates the full message of God with stirring appeal for the heart of every man.

In his writings the full reach of God's saving history from Adam to Christ is profoundly interpreted and brilliantly set forth as an urgent incentive to reach for horizons as vast as God's heavens. The Apostle himself candidly confesses his competence: "To me, the very least of all saints, there was given this grace to announce among the Gentiles the good tidings of the unfathomable riches of Christ, and to enlighten all men as to what is the dispensation of the mystery which has been hidden from eternity in God, who created all things" (Eph. 3:8-9).

If today the Church, the new Israel, hears the thrilling call of God to carry out her vast mission, she hears this through the voice of Paul. If individual members are to share the mind of the Church they too must take Paul as guide. Whatever gains modern biblical study has achieved may all be summed up in the light of Paul's understanding of the saving purpose of God.

What, then, are the focal points of his teaching? To indicate these is the only way of giving point to an essay which is attempting to link modern biblical scholarship with the new horizons opening before us.

Paul teaches clearly that God's saving action must vitalize the whole man and the whole people. Scripture knows nothing of our modern dichotomy of man into soul and body; Scripture is alien to the atomistic individualism of our thinking. God has made man as a personalized and animated body; it is the whole man, therefore, in his physical needs, in his intellectual development, in his social intercourse who belongs to God. Whatever is done for the body is done also for the soul. Whatever benefits man in any way—in his housing, education, status betterment, quite as much as in his spiritual formation—all this can be a vehicle for God's saving action. Our Lord's miracles of giving sight to the blind and health to the sick were true acts of messianic mercy transforming the whole man.

But quite as important, it is man in society who must respond to God. The devout Israelite of old rested all confidence in his membership in the *Qehal Yahweh*. It was in the group fidelity of the whole nation that the devout Israelite of the Old Testament found God's full glory. The integrity of God's people, therefore, was his joy; their sinfulness, his abiding sorrow. The Israel of old has now become the Church. In it all men are to find their perfect fulfillment, and God His full glory. Whatever man can contribute to expand that Church and to extend its influence means the opening up of new areas for God's saving action.

The whole man saved in and through God's whole people; this is God's purpose, the aim of His divine plan.

Paul is a forward-looking man. Like the best of Israel's thinkers, like Christ Himself, Paul envisions a Parousia, a great and manifest coming of the Lord which will consummate all of God's saving interventions upon earth. From his first letter to his last Paul utters a constant "Sursum corda!" Earth is always passing away; the end is near at hand. He so emphasizes this that many have thought he lived in constant expectation of an imminent apocalyptic theophany of God's glory. Whether Paul was ever definitely of this mind we shall never know. If there is urgency in his language it is rather because of his overwhelming certainty of the world's teleology.

For him life is always moving towards the goal of God's final glorification. No matter how much Paul the mystic cherished the riches of Christian life upon earth, no matter how earnestly Paul the apostle labored for the extension of the Church, he never yielded his yearning for the "day of the Lord." This alone spells the consummation of God's saving work and the final triumph of His glory.

In the divine plan, as Paul sees it, man was never intended to walk a treadmill. His every word and action is forward-moving; it marks another step towards the final day, another opportunity to "fill up" the measure of human work which is necessary to prepare for the ultimate glorification of the people whom God has chosen for His glory.

The wonders of the "last day" are not to be understood as a cataclysmic marvel wrought by God alone. The glory of this "day" is rather the completion of a saving work in which man plays a dynamic role. Just as God worked in the human culture of Israel and wrought redemption through the human nature of His son, so He shares with all men the labor of achieving His glory. The resurrection of the whole man on the "last day" is something which man himself is to prepare for; through submission to the transforming influence of the Holy Spirit he is to appropriate the "power of the resurrection" all during life (Phil. 3:10; cf. Rom 8:11). So too the glorification of the people of God and the creation of a new heaven and a new earth must stand as the goal of all human striving. Men of the new Israel are under compelling obligation to contribute as much as possible to the final perfecting of God's work.

This concept gives new perspective to life upon earth. Each talent developed, each career fostered, each advance in technology, each mastery of the world's secret powers, each effort to rehabilitate man and his manners—all this is alight with the glory of the "end-time"; it is man's personal contribution to the final consummation of God's saving work.

All this unfolds a vast horizon, seemingly an unattainable one. This luminous firmament is too high and too distant for man to reach. That is why all through the course of sacred history men have settled for the here and now. Communists are not the only ones whose whole striving is for a realized eschatology bound by the limits of earth. But "the word of our God stands forever" (Is. 40:8). Men must look forward to the day-star of God's full glory and they must march resolutely to the horizon which lies before them.

The third element in Paul's teaching makes this progress not only possible but easy. God has provided the way, and the Way is Christ.

All through the Old Testament God was a Savior. If only the people of Israel had leaned upon Him they would have found Him like a rock in the strength of His support and like an eagle in the tenderness of His mothering care. "You have seen for yourselves," he told them, "how I bore you up on eagle's wings, and brought you here to myself" (Ex. 19:4). What men could not do of themselves God would help them accomplish.

In Christ Jesus "the goodness and kindness of God our Savior appeared" in human flesh (Tit. 3:4). He died and rose again, not merely as an individual but as the true Israel —a corporate personality—bearing to the bosom of His Father the life of every man. If only man says "Yes" to what Christ has done and becomes united to him in Baptism, he becomes one with the Savior as a member engrafted into His body. He begins, therefore, to live through the very power of Christ's Spirit. This means a complete death to sin and an entirely new life in God; this involves a full share in the very death of Christ and in His resurrection.

From the moment of Baptism the whole person of the Christian lives "in Christ Jesus." Whatever he says, whatever he does as a Christian is alive with the power of Christ Himself. From the moment of Baptism, therefore, the Christian becomes a Savior, another Christ, to benefit the whole new Israel, to transform the whole world, and to hasten the Parousia by filtering the light of God's glory into the lives of all men.

Modern biblical scholarship has proven dynamically relevant to the age in which we live. It has uncovered the humanness of God's saving action. He who wrought His wonders in the earthly life of Israel and sent His Son to live a perfectly human life will always be at home in humanness. In men and through men He will continue to save the world and to prepare it for the full manifestation of His glory.

This is why men of all ages have rehearsed the saving deeds of God not merely as memories of the past but as challenges to the present. The saving work of God is to be renewed in every generation and in every human life. Through His power all men are to move steadfastly towards the vast horizons of His full glory.

This has been the constant burden of the Church's teaching in her liturgy. Whatever modern scholarship has achieved of relevance to our own day, this the Church has always taught with beauty and clarity, ever ancient, ever new. Day after day she recounts the words of God and renews in her human worship the dynamic saving *actio* of God. The message of God takes flesh again in the daily celebration of the Church's mysteries. For, in the words of the Secret for the Ninth Sunday after Pentecost, "as often as the Sacrifice is offered, the work of our redemption is renewed."

CHAPTER 2

THE EXODUS,
THEN AND NOW

UPHEAVAL stirred the world of Abraham. Dynastic changes at Ur and vast migrations over the Fertile Crescent stirred the stagnant pool of a world that had died. Babylon in the early second millennium boasted, "I am rich and have grown wealthy and have need of nothing"; and all the while the bragging corpse failed to see how "wretched and miserable and poor and blind and naked" it really was (Apoc. 3:17). All flesh had corrupted its way; God's clean sun shone on a pool full of death.

But life still throbbed at Haran in northern Mesopotamia, for Abraham lived there, a newcomer from Ur in the south. All future history would flow from him; he was to become "the father of us all . . . our father in the sight of God" (Rom. 4:17). For one day at Haran, in the middle of the nineteenth century before Christ, God spoke to the heart of this tribal chief (Gen. 12:1-3) and broke it wide open with a freshet of mercy, which gushed forth to cleanse all hearts by faith.

The divine word promised a blessed future, without telling its precise elements or the time of its coming. Long centuries were to pass before this pledge was fulfilled. But the very sound of God's voice is operative, never returning to Him empty, always doing His will (Is. 55:10-11); hardly had He spoken when His promise began to send forth clean water that spread out in ever-widening circles of mercy and loving fidelity until it covered the earth (*cf.,* Ez. 47:1-12). The mercy of God touching each generation performs a univocal work of redeeming from death and of invigorating with life, so that all successive moments of history follow the same pattern: the wide outer circle of Christian fulfillment is of the same form as the small inner circle of God's promise to Abraham; and all the circles between bear similar shape. Thus a vital continuity binds fast the story of salvation; far from opposing the Old Testament, the New Testament, to use the apt phrase of Père de Vaux, "prolongs it."

It must be so, for God has shaped all to the full measure of His Christ. Through Him the waters of divine mercy were to touch all shores; and so, the vast outer circle of mercy's world-wide expansion gives form to every inner circle, even to the first circle of the water's origin in the heart of Abraham. Christ's redeeming death is at once the cause and the pattern of every previous deed of divine mercy. Typology, then—mighty deeds foreshadowing mightier to come—inheres in the Old Testament as a necessary consequence of the Christian quality of all God's work. In His great deeds for Israel, God so kept His Son in mind that Soren Kierkegaard could speak of "the eternal contemporaneousness of Christ"; and the Master Himself could say, "Abraham your father rejoiced that he was to see my day. He saw it and was glad" (Jn. 8:56).

This living bond between the Old and New Testaments

is best exemplified in the vital typology of Israel's exodus from Egypt. The event was of supreme importance, for it played a unique creative role in forming the nation, in fashioning its faith and way. Ever afterward Israel commemorated it with the annual Passover feast, when men recounted at local shrines and family tables the stirring tale of their deliverance. Its memory was handed down from father to son in streams of tradition marked with all the divergences and accretions of oral history often recounted. Thus even today the biblical story of the Exodus, carefully wrought as it is, betrays unmistakable signs of sundry threads deftly woven into a single pattern. Yet the basic historicity of the narrative cannot be questioned; it is an authentic witness to real events that marked the birth of Israel as a nation and of the worship of Yahweh. Memory is tenacious in the East; and, in this case, its reliability is certified by the fact that Israel was often tempted to forget the story of its origin and the stern exactions of Yahweh, its God.

Here is the story simply told. Some seventeen centuries before Christ, a group of Hebrews driven by famine descended into Egypt where they enjoyed favor under the new dynasty of the Hyksos kings, who had recently swept into power on the wave of a vast Semite migration of which Abraham was part. These sons of Jacob were to remain in the Delta four hundred years, not as a nation within a nation but as an ethnic group, Hebrew in blood but Egyptian in sentiment. Life in the foreign land soiled them with pagan ways and practices. They prospered in this world's goods and in its evils; idolatry came easily and Egyptian manners were to their liking. But at last the long, peaceful sojourn in Egypt changed to a burdensome existence under cruel persecution. Too long had Israel thickened on its lees; and now, through a tyrannical Pharaoh, God poured the oversweet wine from vessel to vessel.

A native Egyptian dynasty stripped the Hebrews of all privileges and shackled them with the burdens of an unwelcome minority. This persecution is the first instance of cruel anti-Semitism described in the Bible. Cries of pain and despair rent the air; and God answered. He made ready a man of the hour, whose name was Moses. Native gifts and early training equipped him for leadership. But the forging of bonds between God and men is more than a human task. First, then, God Himself had to temper the mettle of His instrument. Years of exile with the Kenites in the rocky land southwest of the Dead Sea enriched his mind with new traditions and new insights. But, more important still, these years purified his soul for that contact which God would make with him in a flame of fire at Sinai.

Time and again God had manifested Himself to the great patriarchs of Israel—Abraham, Isaac, and Jacob. This time, however, God's word pulsed with new meaning. Truly it was still the great *El Shaddai* of the fathers who spoke to Moses. Yet now this most high God, the God of heaven and earth, asked for a special bond with Israel. Later the prophets were to liken this bond to the tie that binds husband and wife; in their eyes this blood covenant made Israel the people of God and God the spouse and master of Israel (Jer. 3:1-12; Ez. 16). But for Moses on Sinai God's command involved the here and now. For at Sinai God charged him to lead the people out of Egypt, to shepherd them through the desert, and to bring them into the land He had promised to their fathers.

It was a mammoth task to ask of any man. Yet God, who was both solicitous and powerful, promised to help Moses. His new name was a guarantee. For He would no longer be called merely the great *El Shaddai* of the nations; He would be *Yahweh,* the faithful God of their own covenant. Whether Moses first heard this name among the Kenites, or whether it was newly revealed to him at Sinai, matters little. Its meaning it what counts. "I am he who is," God assured Moses. He is always the mysterious "I am," an alien to the shift of human gods from past to future. And so Yahweh—"He who is"—would always be present among His people. His name would be a prayer on the lips of the people, a promise when spoken by God.

It required centuries for Israel to taste the full flavor of the Sinai revelation and to understand how the name Yahweh was at once the source of all fear and of all hope. Suffering must first bring God's people to wisdom; the prophets must first see their visions. Then, at long last, the Sinai revelation of God's unfailing mercy would become a conviction. Whatever Israel might do, Yahweh will never turn from the mercy and promise of Sinai. He will always be faithful and true; pity and fidelity will rule all His works (Ps. 24:10). When Israel ceased being a child and grew to spiritual maturity, it came to see that, even from the beginning of the world, God had always been the selfsame, cherishing His creatures, as a nurse her little ones, with mercy and fidelity. Then it could appreciate the full meaning of Osee's urgent plea, "The Lord, the God of hosts, the Lord is His name! You shall return by the help of your God, if you remain loyal and do right and always hope in your God" (Os. 12:6-7).

It was the memory of the Exodus that did most to convince Israel of God's power and pity. At the time, men saw it simply as a liberation from the hard oppression of Pharaoh; but later they came to appreciate it also as a liberation from the worse evil of defilement by Egyptian infidelity and idolatry. Indeed, the prophetic school looked upon the deliverance as a true redemption, with God as a warrior, struggling in desperate conflict with Pharaoh and the dragon power of his gods (Is. 51:9-10). One after another Yahweh hurled His ten plagues against a king's proud heart that only hardened like mud under the burning heat of the divine bolts. But the last plague was a master stroke, not softening Pharaoh's heart, but breaking it in helpless defeat. Where flood and storm and hail had failed, the death of the first-born cleaved the rock.

All through the terrors, the sons of Jacob were spared; the plagues struck all around them, but they were untouched. Their preservation from God's final blow involved the ritual of the paschal supper and a ceremony of smearing blood on the doorposts. The incidents of this last night in Egypt burned a lasting memory in the soul of Israel. The contrast between their security and the anguish of the Egyptians, the change of heart in obdurate Pharaoh, and the urgent pleadings of their Egyptian neighbors that the Hebrews enrich themselves from previously hoarded treasures —all this forced upon them the recognition of Yahweh's special favor. Ever before, Egypt had shared its riches with Israel's patriarchs, Abraham, Jacob, and Joseph. But the sons of Jacob came out of the darkness of the paschal night with something far better than Egypt's gold and fine linen; they departed from the land under Moses' leadership with a new consciousness that God had carved them out from the heart of an alien race to become His own special people. Yahweh was with them as their God, and the fiery cloud of the Shekinah leading them was His symbol.

The Exodus was only half of God's work. He had delivered His people from bondage and separated them from the contamination of Egypt. A positive task yet remained:

to forge a bond of union and weld Israel to Himself with a covenant of blood. Like all union with God, this could be done only in the desert. "I will lead her into the desert," the Lord was later to say of Israel, the unfaithful, "and I will speak to her heart" (Os. 2:16). The *Shekinah* therefore, diverted the line of march from the Via Maris, the direct route to the promised land, and turned southward instead to the region of Sinai.

But Israel's problems with Pharaoh were not yet over; very shortly the king's retainers set out in hot pursuit to bring back the fugitives. And Israel would have gone back readily if God had not intervened with a definitive liberation that once for all swept it out beyond Pharaoh's reach. The story of the miracle is one of the most stirring in the Bible. The fleeing people found itself in a cul-de-sac: on one side the Red Sea, on the other and behind them the mountains, in front the approaching Egyptians. There was no escape save in surrender—or in God. And God intervened. Moses lifted the rod; and a driving wind parted the waters for Israel to march across to safety. The Egyptians followed; but once more Moses lifted his rod; and the waters returned to destroy them all. Israel could not miss the meaning of the wonder; they sang and danced to honor the merciful Yahweh, their God. In the words of Dom Damasus Winzen, this jubilant song marks "the hour when the Divine Office was born"; it is the seed of the Church's solemn praise of God.

Indeed, Yahweh was always at hand to supply the needs of the child He had found languishing and had mercifully freed. Time and again on this journey He proved to an incredulous people that it was really He who had intervened to point their destiny. When they were thirsty, He struck water from the rock; when they were hungry, He provided bread from heaven. Therefore, when at last this people reached Sinai, they already had ample experience of God's solicitude and power.

They needed these previous love tokens, for Sinai was the scene of espousals that bound Israel to Yahweh forever. The thunder and lightning of the theophany were terrifying; the ritual of covenant was detailed and impressive; but a love story was the heart of it all. Yahweh bound Himself to Israel and Israel to Yahweh in a covenant of blood. He on His part would love and protect Israel and fulfill the rich promises He had pledged; Israel would ever live and act as His people, faithfully fulfilling the just and holy house rules of a God who was perfect. Just as in Egypt God's word had delivered the bodies of His people from Pharaoh, so on Sinai the word of God delivered their souls from the darkness of unbelief and evil practice. Israel is thus a people created by God's word; moreover, its very continuance depended on divine promises and demands.

Ever after, Israel looked back to the Exodus and to the Sinai pact as the birth hour of the nation. Its history was often marred by infidelities, but no weakness of man could obliterate three dominant factors which Sinai burned into the Israelite soul: there is but one God; one chosen people; one country in which to work out the people's destiny. It was especially the yearly celebration of the Passover feast that kept this national memory intact (*cf.* Ex. 12:14). With Israel, the Passover was not a nature feast commemorating the return of spring, as with the surrounding Canaanites. Rather, it was a religious feast, to recall the springtime of God's favor when through the Exodus, He graciously ended the winter of oppression and, at Sinai, entered on the bright joyous days of His espousals with Israel.

All memories of these incidents are steeped in praise and thanksgiving; later generations will sing of the Exodus as of a triumph (Ps. 104, 113) and of the covenant of Sinai as an espousals in which God chose Israel for Himself. As time passed, the importance of the Exodus grew to full stature in the minds of men; and its profound meaning was richly interpreted in the sweeping poetry of the prophets and the Deuteronomist. All later laws of the priestly code were traced to Sinai; and the definitive redaction of the Pentateuch after the Exile rested the authority of its laws on the authority of Moses.

But there was a twofold orientation in Israel's faith. It centered in the historical exodus which had passed, but it looked forward also to an exodus yet to come. The reason is obvious. God had promised a full flowering, and the merciful pledge of Yahweh, the faithful One, is without repentance. Yet daily events brought bitter experience that the deliverance from Egypt and the covenant of Sinai were not definitive. Time and again Israel hankered for the fleshpots of Egypt; and only too often, like Gomer, the wife of Osee, it proved unfaithful to its faithful Spouse.

From the very beginning, then, the prophets saw that there had to be a new exodus and a new covenant (*cf.*, Os. 2:16-25). This enduring hope enriched the memory of Israel's deliverance from Egypt and its covenant with God on Sinai. For the prophets, these events of the past were unforgettable historical facts, but even more they were cherished pledges of a blessed future.

It was Christ who fulfilled all the rich hopes of the prophets. His very name held promise; for, as the angel explained to Joseph, this name was at once a symbol and a guarantee that, at long last, Yahweh had come to save His people (Mt. 1:31). It was but natural, then, that the writers of the New Testament should find in Israel's exodus from Egypt a leitmotiv for their own description of the work of Christ. Steeped as they were in the Scriptures, these men tended to locate the Savior in the biblical context of the great deliverance. The word "exodus," as used by them, always resounds with the full meaning of that historic event.

Often enough there is striking agreement among all the Evangelists in handling the elements of this typology; such identifications were probably fixed and made permanent in the oral catechesis which preceded the writing of the Gospels. Yet, at the same time, there is also marked fluidity; Jesus is variously identified with the God of the Exodus, with Israel itself, with Moses the leader, or with the chief factor in some incident of the Exodus. Such divergence should occasion no surprise; for all these different aspects merely stress that the basic typology of Exodus must be sought in the mercy and fidelity of a saving God who, in solicitude for Israel, penetrated every person, event, and thing with His own divine power. Each element in the story of the Exodus foreshadowed the much greater work of Christian redemption in which divine power penetrated the human nature and human deeds of Jesus, to work a definitive liberation from sin and an eternal covenant with God. Therefore, in pondering the many Gospel applications of Exodus typology, we come to a new, rich appreciation of the perfect deliverance that God wrought in and through Jesus.

Among the Synoptics, the Gospel of St. Matthew is especially rich with this typology. The avowed purpose of the author of the first Gospel was to stress the continuity between the Old and the New Law. It is obvious, then, that he would utilize the widespread Jewish expectation that "in the last days" God must work a new exodus. In developing this theme, Matthew like Mark stresses a similarity between the experiences of Christ and those of the chosen people of God. Thus the return of the holy family from Egypt, after the death of Herod, is seen by Matthew as a new exodus; and so he captions it with the very words Osee had used to describe the earlier event: "Out of Egypt I called my son" (Mt. 2:15; Os. 11:1). The beginnings of the Savior's public life are also linked to similar incidents in the history of Israel. As Israel was baptized into its new life with God by passing through the waters of the Red Sea, so Christ inaugurates His ministry for God by accepting baptism in the waters of the Jordan (Mt. 3:13-17; Mk. 1:9-11). Thereafter both Israel and Christ live through a period of desert life and temptation. The forty days of Christ in the desert has its parallel in the forty years of Israel; His temptation accords with Israel's testing; His food is the word of God that comes down from heaven, just as Israel's food in the desert is not the bread of man's making but the manna of God's giving (Mt. 4:1-11; Mk. 1:12-13). It is especially noteworthy that Christ defeats His tempter with texts from the book of Deuteronomy, all of them summing up the wisdom of God that guided and strengthened Israel.

After this early identification of Christ with Israel, Matthew prefers to emphasize the resemblance between Christ and Moses. Generalizations are, of course, always a risk. But there is some justification for saying that Matthew's chief concern is to represent Christ as a second Moses, greater by far than the first lawgiver of Israel. The keynote of this identification is sounded in Matthew's representation of Christ's first discourse, the Sermon on the Mount (Mt. 5-7). As Moses drafted the law of the Old Covenant, so Christ presents here the law of the New. This law is perfect in every way; and Christ Himself is a law-giver of divine holiness and authority. As a master He handles the earlier law with deft touch, changing at will and fashioning to perfection. God had spoken through Moses; but this new Moses is more than an instrument, infinitely more than the mouthpiece of God. And so "the crowds were astonished at His teaching; for He was teaching them as one having authority" (Mt. 7:28-29).

This resemblance between the two lawgivers dominates all the later discourses of Jesus in the first Gospel; indeed, the Master draws largely from Deuteronomy for the expression of His own thoughts. Moreover, there is likeness even in Christ's method of teaching. His soul, like that of Moses, was a limpid pool reflecting divine truth without distortion; in both men passion was controlled; nothing disturbed their tranquil grasp of truth or marred the clarity of its expression. For God said of Moses, "Moses was by far the meekest man on the face of the earth" (Num. 12:3), just as Christ said of Himself, "Learn from me, for I am meek and humble of heart" (Mt. 11:29).

The wonders and miracles of Christ also point a likeness between Himself and Moses. Through both lawgivers God wrought mighty works to authenticate their mission and to win for their law a hearing. It is not the meaning of the miracle that interests Matthew, nor its resemblance in kind to the miracles of Moses. Thus he is content to tell the story of the multiplication of the loaves without referring, as John does, to the profound symbolism of bread coming miraculously from heaven. Matthew's concern is with the fact itself. Miracles are God's own work as He had wrought wonders through Moses, so now He was working in Jesus. Both were lawgivers mighty not only in word but also in deed.

It is especially in describing the Transfiguration that both

Matthew and Mark bring into focus the typology of Moses (Mt. 17:1-8; Mk. 9:1-7). Here the two great lawgivers of Old Covenant and New meet face to face; and the bright cloud that once overshadowed Moses (Ex. 33:9-10) now descends upon Jesus. Heaven's authentication of the new Moses follows the pattern of its approval of the old.

The author of the fourth Gospel is even more pointed in showing how Christ fulfilled the typology of Israel's exodus from Egypt. In fact, some have suggested that Exodus provides the whole framework of this Gospel, and that John follows it step by step to prove that Jesus, as a new Moses and a new Lamb of God, came upon earth to lead a new Israel from the oppression of sin to the liberty of a new covenant with God. It is difficult to accept this thesis in its entirety; for in a Gospel of so many themes it is an oversimplification to reduce all to a single unity. But the fact remains that the Exodus motif is prevalent in the fourth Gospel.

Like Matthew, John too marks a resemblance between Christ and the lawgiver of Israel. But his arm is to evoke all the richness of the Exodus typology; for he is not only a witness to the Gospel tradition, but even more its "inspired exegete." Therefore, in his treatment of the life and work of Christ, many new aspects of similarity appear.

Often enough he is content merely to suggest a point of resemblance. Thus four times in this Gospel Jesus appropriates to Himself the divine name first revealed to Moses at Horeb (Jn. 8:24, 28, 58; 13:19); but in all these instances the reference to the Sinai revelation is allusive rather than explicit. So, too, there is passing reference to the new espousals that will bring to perfection the old covenant (Jn. 3:29-30). But after the brief, unadorned words of John the Baptist, this theme too is dropped.

Other points of resemblance, however, are emphasized

and developed at length. The chief of these is the Paschal
Lamb motif. It was the blood of the unblemished lamb that
saved the first-born of Israel from slaughter and made possible the departure for the promised land. In John's eyes,
Christ is the true Lamb of God who shed His blood on
Calvary to save men from the death of sin and to liberate
them for the promised land of heaven. John's first introduction to Christ was the Baptist's salute "Behold the
Lamb of God!" (Jn. 1:36). Ever after, this typology
loomed large in the mind of the Evangelist. Thus several
times he makes a deliberate effort to connect Jesus' death
with the feast of the Passover (Jn. 2:13; 6:4; 11:55); the
providential coincidence of time between the paschal celebration and the death of Christ on the cross provided him
an opportunity to stress an underlying typology. Perhaps
there is also a meaningful play in John's introduction to
his account of the Last Supper: "Before the feast of the
Passover, Jesus, knowing that His hour had come to pass
out of the world to the Father . . ." (Jn. 13:1). Certainly
there is a deliberate allusion to the ritual of the paschal
celebration in John's remark that no bone of the Victim on
the cross was broken (Jn. 19:36). It is obvious, then, even
to a casual reader of the fourth Gospel that John found in
the lamb of Egypt a memorable type of the later Lamb of
Israel.

He finds also many other resemblances. For him, Christ
is the light of the world (Jn. 8:12). The conflict between
this light and the surrounding darkness is a favorite theme
with John. But this theme is not his own; its source is
biblical. He has drawn it from the beautiful contemplative
meditations of the author of the Wisdom of Solomon who
penetrates the deep truths contained in God's guiding care
of His people as He went before them on their journey,

lighting the way with the glory of the *Shekinah*. A cloud of divine light led Israel from Egypt to the promised land; this was the visible sign of God's presence with His people. For St. John, Jesus is the true light of the world, for He is the Word of God dwelling among men and radiating everywhere the "glory of the Only-Begotten of the Father, full of grace and truth" (Jn. 1:14). Men must follow this light if they would reach their heavenly home safely; they must approach and love this light if they desire divine approval (Jn. 3:19-21). Thus the Evangelist's witness to Christ as the guiding light of men is hardly appreciated unless one sees it against the biblical context of the *Shekinah* of the Exodus.

The manna from heaven was yet another element of Israel's exodus which St. John utilized as a type of Christ's beneficent action. In this identification the Evangelist was not original, for Jewish exegesis itself had already given to the manna an eschatological meaning. Devout Israelites were certain that, as God nourished their fathers with bread from heaven in the desert, so He would nourish them with heavenly food in the "last days"; they were certain that the manna would reappear in messianic times. This Jewish belief is indicated in the questions the crowd put to Jesus (Jn. 6:30-31). John himself relies on this tradition when, in his book of revelation, he equates manna and the tree of life as perfect symbols of the divine goods to be shared by the blessed in the world to come (Apoc. 2:7, 17). It was the precise object of the fourth Gospel to show that this eschatological food is already given to the Church; it is hers here and now because of the abiding presence of Jesus in the vital and life-giving reality of the Eucharist. If, as some have thought, the component parts of John's Gospel originated as elements of the primitive sacramental catechesis, then it is obvious that the typology of the manna was widely used in the early Church to describe the riches of the Eucharist.

But in the desert wanderings, God not only fed His people but also provided water for them from the rock. John follows Paul (1 Cor. 10:4) in identifying this rock of Sinai as a type of Christ. This theme of refreshing spiritual water is stressed in John even more than the manna. His use of this type reflects its prevalence in the baptismal catechesis of the early Church and also in the catechetical instructions on grace and spiritual life. It is true that the baptismal reference made by Christ in His discourse with Nicodemus (Jn. 3:5) is probably based on Israel's baptism in the waters of the Red Sea and in the cloud, as touched on by Paul in 1 Cor. 10:1-2; but elsewhere in the fourth Gospel the theme of water seems to rest on the typology of the drink provided miraculously by God in the desert. Christ is the true rock from whom all life and all refreshment must come.

The brazen serpent, too, figures in the fourth Gospel as a type of the healing power of Christ's redemption: "As Moses lifted up the serpent in the desert, even so must the Son of Man be lifted up" (Jn. 3:14). These words of Christ are a bare allusion to the miraculous cure wrought by God for His people (Num. 21:9). But, in the light of Wisdom 16:5-13, this brief sentence crystallizes a rich typology to provide John with a point of departure for his sublime theology of redemption (Jn. 3:14-21). In his pages type and fulfillment are so intimately interwoven that they mutually interact to aid the mind in penetrating the wealth of each.

All in all, the story of Christ as told in the Gospels is understood when it is read in the biblical context of Israel's

exodus. For Matthew, Mark, and John were all true Israelites, steeped in the Scriptures and sharing Israel's hope
for an ineffable renewal of the divine mercy that led the
chosen people out of Egypt, bequeathed a covenant on
Sinai, and made good its pledge of loving devotedness by
working wonders to hearten Israel during the desert wanderings. Long before the Evangelists appeared, the Jews
had seen in the events of the Exodus shadows cast before-
hand by a blessed future. It is the merit of the Evangelists
that they found in Christ the perfect fulfillment of all the
Old Testament hopes—the "substance" that had cast out
the shadows (Col. 2:17).

The life and work of Christ are not over. Before He died,
the Savior promised to abide with His Church always—ever
the same Christ, "yesterday, today, yes, and forever" (Heb.
13:8). Strong is the bond between Moses and Israel, but
stronger still, intimate as no other, is the union which binds
Christ to His people in the Church. For the new Moses
and the new Israel are joined together as head and members
of one mystical body, as bridegroom and bride of a true
marriage. In the mystery of His Church, Christ is personally present to every age and renders accessible to every
follower the very substance of His life and work upon earth.
As St. Leo the Great expressed it: "What was visible in our
Redeemer during His earthly sojourn has now passed into
the sacraments." Though the Church is the Church of
pilgrimage, traveling toward the great Day of the Lord;
though she moves in time, waiting, hoping, and praying,
"Thy kingdom come," she stands all through time on an
atemporal level. She is the tremendous Sacrament that
brings the Christ of the first century into every age and into
every heart. For "each time the mysteries are renewed, the
work of redemption becomes actual once more." What

was wrought in Jesus during His earthly life is renewed in the soul of every Christian. Christ's mysteries belong to His Church and to each member, not merely to contemplate and to utilize but also to relive.

The exodus of Israel from Egypt, therefore, does not exhaust its theology in prefiguring Christ's redeeming life, death, and resurrection. By the very fact that it fore-shadowed the events of His life, it also prefigured the life of His followers, who would be Israel renewed. For the daily life of Christ's mystical body is but the living repro-duction and fulfillment of the saving mysteries in the life of Christ Himself. This is the reason according to Henri de Lubac, S.J., why "the typology of Exodus is the most classic and constant in our liturgical tradition and in Christian literature."

The patristic catecheses which formed the Christian mind place the origin of a Christian's spiritual life at the moment when, through Baptism, he shares in the liberating death of the true Paschal Lamb. Like Israel of old, he is thereby delivered from slavery to the devil; he becomes a member of "a chosen race, a royal priesthood, a holy nation, a purchased people" (1 Pet. 2:9). As the years pass and he journeys through the desert of this life, the Christian finds in the mighty activity of Christ a kindliness, a divine mercy supporting him all his days and leading him to the promised land of heaven (cf., Is. 46:3f; Heb. 1:3). But the passing from the death of sin to the vibrant life of heaven must be accomplished in Christ—through the power of His exodus, in His company, and according to the pattern of His ex-ample. For the exodus and desert journey of the Christian involves both a sacramental sharing in the mystery of Christ and a vital imitation of His conduct.

It was natural, then, for the early Fathers to emphasize

the biblical foundation of the sacramental signs. Just as
St. John showed how the redemptive work of Christ renewed and enriched the great wonders of the Exodus, so
the Fathers taught that the Christian sacraments, as living
instruments of the Passion, continue these wonders and
apply them, with new divine power and new Christian
meaning, to every believer. In this they remained true to
the primitive symbolism of the sacraments, which was taken
directly from Israel's liturgy and the typology of the Old
Testament. Humanly speaking there could be no other
source, for Christ and His apostles had been schooled only
in the traditions of Israel. Afterwards, it is true, writers
of Greek background tried to explain the sacramental symbolism in a new way; new meanings were borrowed from
the thoughts and customs of a Greek world. And all this
has helped to enrich man's appreciation of the sacraments.
But their primitive meaning must still be studied in the light
of a biblical context.

The early Fathers of the Church were careful to preserve
this biblical foundation of the sacramental signs. Thus
their thought on Baptism was always controlled by St.
Paul's identification of its type in the crossing of the Red
Sea (1 Cor. 10:2). For him, the exodus from Egypt and
the passage through the Sea prefigured the deliverance from
evil that comes to the Christian through Baptism. The two
realities have similar meanings; each marks, in its own way,
the end of servitude and the beginning of a new existence.

Again, this thought is not original with Paul. For at the
beginning of the Christian era, the initiation of proselytes
into the Jewish community included not only circumcision
but also Baptism, in imitation of the exodus from Egypt
through the parted waters of the Red Sea. This symbolic
act was charged with the redemptive power of Christ to

become a true sacrament of the New Law. What was merely commemorative with the Jews became dynamically operative with the Christians. The ritual washing became a vital sharing in the deliverance from sin and the birth to new life achieved by Christ's exodus on the cross: "Do you not know that all we who have been baptized into Christ Jesus have been baptized into His death? For we were buried with Him by means of baptism into death, in order that, just as Christ has arisen from the dead through the glory of the Father, so we also may walk in newness of life" (Rom. 6:3f).

With the Fathers, then, the exodus of Israel from Egypt was a type not only of Christ's death but also of Christian Baptism. For them the Old Testament contained both a christological and a sacramental typology. The baptismal catechesis of Tertullian is especially eloquent: "When the people, set unconditionally free, escaped the violence of the Egyptian king by crossing over through water, it was water that exterminated the king himself, with his entire force. What figure is more manifestly fulfilled in the sacrament of baptism? The nations are set free from the world by means of water; and the devil, their old tyrant, they leave behind, overwhelmed in the water."

This passage places in focus the primitive perspective of Baptism and redemption. Both were seen, above all, as a victory over the demon. On the cross, Christ crushed His adversary's head to liberate all humanity from the cruel yoke of sin; and each Christian shares in this triumph of Christ at the moment of Baptism. The waters of Baptism annihilate Satan's power as completely as the Red Sea drowned the forces of Pharaoh. The deliverance wrought by God for the Israelites in freeing them forever through water from an earthly tyrant and in leading them out as a new nation into the desert finds its antitype in Baptism, which liberates a spiritual people from a spiritual tyrant and leads them from the world to the kingdom of God. This theme is frequent in the baptismal catecheses of the Fathers.

A striking example is this passage by St. Cyril of Jerusalem:

> Needs must you know that the type of baptism is found in Israel's ancient history. Indeed, when Pharaoh, the bitter and savage tyrant, oppressed the free and noble people of the Hebrews, God sent Moses to free them from the evil Egyptian bondage. The doorposts were daubed with the blood of the lamb so that the destroying angel would pass over the houses marked with the sign of blood. Thus, against all hope, the Hebrew people was set free. As the enemy pursued the liberated, however, he saw, marvelous to say, the sea divided for them; he was avidly going after them, treading in their footsteps, when he was forthwith swallowed by the floods of the Red Sea and buried there. Let us move now from things ancient to things new, from type to reality. There we have Moses sent by God into Egypt, here we have the Christ sent by the Father into the world. There it was in order to free the oppressed people from Egypt, here it is to rescue men tyrannized in this world by sin. There the blood of the lamb warded off the destroyer, here the blood of Jesus Christ, the immaculate Lamb, puts the demons to flight. There the tyrant pursued that ancient people even to the sea, here the shameless and insolent prince of all evil gives chase even to the very brink of the sacred font. The one was drowned in the sea, the other is brought to nothing in the saving water.

The Exodus provided also a sublime typology for the Eucharist. Here, too, the Fathers drew largely from the primitive sacramental catechesis reflected in the pages of the New Testament. The inspired authors had seized on

two elements in the Exodus story as prefigurements of the
nourishing and strengthening presence of Christ. St. John
favored the manna; St. Paul, the rock of Sinai. Both symbols were eloquent of the solicitous and operative providence of Emmanuel. It was only to be expected, then, that
the manna-rock symbolism would become a dominant element in patristic teaching. Time and again, in explaining
the reality and effects of the Eucharist, the Fathers return
to these types as divinely ordained prefigurements of Holy
Communion.

Indeed, the Fathers utilized all the elements of christological typology in the Exodus story as an equivalent sacramental typology. Thus the very liturgy of initiation, because
it took place in the paschal period, is charged with remi-
niscences of the exodus from Egypt. Each factor in that
historical event was identified as a type of the exodus
achieved by Christ through His way of the cross and shared
in sacramentally by each Christian through his participation
in the Christian mysteries.

But something more than a sacramental share in Christ's
Passover is demanded of the Christian. For the sacrament
gives grace; and grace means immanent activity. All initiation, therefore, into the mystery of Christ must be accompanied by a conversion of morals and by vital Christian
living, a duty St. Paul never tired of insisting on. After
recounting all that God had done for Israel in the desert,
he warned his converts: "Now these things happened to
them as a type, and they were written for our correction,
upon whom the final age of the world has come" (1 Cor.
10:11). The same lessons are stressed in the Epistle to the
Hebrews (3:1-4:13). There the typology of the Old Testament points to positive cooperation, demands of the followers of Christ an eager striving for goodness, a hastening
toward the promised land.

The Fathers were unanimous in repeating these inspired demands. All were enemies of a sacramentary quietism, with its contempt for the sweat and toil of moral effort and its search for a rest in God which is not for man the pilgrim—a doctrine condemned again by Pope Pius XII in his encyclical *Mediator Dei*. They insisted that the Christian's sacramental share in Christ's Passover brought a new vital power which must be exercised in daily Christian living. Christ's exodus traced the way of the cross; the way of the cross, then, dying to self, is the only authentic Christian exodus: "Unto this, indeed, you have been called, because Christ also has suffered for you, leaving you an example that you may follow in His steps" (1 Pet. 2:21). St. John Chrysostom gives pointed expression to this patristic teaching in one of his homilies. This is his thought: The Lord had brought the Israelites out of Egypt, and, yet, except for a few, they grumbled against Him, mistrusted His might, doubted His love. Therefore they were barred from setting foot in the Holy Land, and the grace of liberation and safe passage through the Red Sea availed them nothing. In like wise, it avails a Christian nothing to have received Baptism and to have shared in the spiritual mysteries, unless he leads a life worthy of this grace.

Truly, the Exodus is not an event of the past. Though in Christ we are indeed delivered from sin, from idolatry, and from death, we must be ever in exodus, ever passing over, ever leaving behind the servitude of idolatrous Egypt, ever marching through the austerity of the desert, ever doing our utmost to enter the promised land. Till the day of Christ's return, we, God's people, remain as it were in the wilderness. There is still the yearning for Egypt's ease; still the crowd murmurs, still leaders sin. Yet God is faithful and, chastening and forgiving, thrusts us forward without fail toward the new heaven and the new earth which Jesus will usher in when He comes again. Thus to be saved, one must take the road God showed to Israel, one must walk the stations of the cross. For Israel's route is the route of the whole of God's people and of each one of them.

Christian life fulfills the typology of Israel's Exodus because it is a life in Christ and a full sharing in His wondrous mysteries. But the redeeming mission of the Savior does not reach its consummation in this world; and so life here below cannot be the final fulfillment of the types God prepared in the Old Law. Only heaven can provide that.

It is the privilege of St. John, then, to speak the last word in the glorious pages of his Apocalypse. There he describes the full flowering of all that Exodus typology promised, of all that Christ accomplished. The whole heavenly scene is dominated by the victorious Lamb; it is His blood that has achieved all; through Him the wonders of the first exodus reach their crown. The elect who have crossed the Red Sea of death sing anew the victory song of Moses and Miriam (Apoc. 15:2-3). The covenant between God and His people is final and perfect; the new Israel has become God's bride, and "God Himself will be with them as their God" (Apoc. 21:3). To him who thirsts God gives "the water of life freely" (Apoc. 21:6); to him who is hungry He gives "the hidden manna" (Apoc. 2:17). Forever the Israel of heaven shall be "a kingdom and priests"; and all shall sing with joy the canticle of the Lamb: "To Him who has loved us and washed us from our sins in His own blood, and made us to be a kingdom, and priests to God His Father—to Him belong glory and dominion forever and ever. Amen" (Apoc. 1:5-6).

The exodus of Israel, the exodus of Christ, the exodus of the Christian—all form a vital unity, all compenetrate in perfect harmony. The Israel of old, mindful of God's mercy in the first exodus, prayed ardently for a richer renewal: "Shepherd your people with your staff, the flock of your inheritance. . . . As in the days when you came from the land of Egypt, show us wonderful signs" (Mich. 7:14f). God heard this prayer, and granted the "wonderful signs" of Christ's redemption. This second exodus is greater by far than the first; yet consummation follows the pattern of promise. Both are mighty works of God, revealing His power and His person in the concord of a blended minor and major scale. One cannot be appreciated without the other; both scales sound true only in their mighty harmony.

This fact is fundamental to Christian theology; it is no less essential to Christian spirituality. Pascal achieved his supreme mystical experience in that night of prayer in which he glimpsed how truly the God of Abraham, Isaac, and Jacob was his own God. So, too, every Christian who would really live his Christian life must come to realize that the God of Israel at the Red Sea, the God of Jesus on Calvary, the God of every Christian on earth, the God of the glorified Israel in heaven is always one and the same— "yesterday, today, yes, and forever" (Heb. 13:8).

CHAPTER 3 THE SPIRIT
OF THE
OLD TESTAMENT
SAINTS

THERE was a day at Nazareth—before she was known as "Queen" or "Mediatrix"—when Mary was simply a lovely young Jewess and nothing more. Faithful child of Abraham and daughter of David, she belonged, mind and heart, to those who waited expectantly to welcome the Messiah.

Her inner life followed a pattern traced by the prophets for the holy remnant of Israel. Prophets had dreamed wondrous dreams of this little group offering to the Messiah the faith of Israel's patriarchs, the desires of her seers, the holiness of her just ones. But it is the prophet Sophonia who has expressed best of all the spirit of the chosen remnant. His eyes alight with vision, he promised in the name of God:

> I will leave as a remnant in your midst
>   a people humble and lowly,
> Who shall take refuge in the name of the Lord:
>   the remnant of Israel.
> They shall do no wrong
>   and speak no lies;

> Nor shall there be found in their mouths
>   a deceitful tongue; . . .
> On that day it shall be said to Jerusalem:
>   Fear not, O Sion, be not discouraged!
> The Lord, your God, is in your midst,
>   A mighty savior;
> He will rejoice over you with gladness,
>   and renew you in his love,
> He will sing joyfully because of you,
>   as one sings at festivals.
>
> (Soph. 3:12f, 16f)

Mary of Nazareth belonged to this "people, humble and lowly" her soul steeped as no other in their spirit of trusting dependence. To learn the riches of her inward life, the thoughts that filled her mind and the secrets of her heart, is to study what it meant to be one of Israel's *anawim*— God's "humble and lowly."

The concept of the *anawim* has roots in the earth that was "waste and void"; it originated in the primeval darkness which covered the abyss when "the spirit of God was stirring above the waters" (Gen. 1:2). At that moment God worked on nothing to produce all that is; and, when finished, "God saw that all he had made was very good" (1:31). God at work on nothing to produce all that is good: this is the record of every divine deed in Israel's history.

The very origin of this people as the children of Abraham called for a miracle, the birth of Isaac from an aged father and mother. It was always the same: God was ever at work to make Israel what He wanted it to be. For some it was merely a turn of chance that prepared the land of Egypt for the long sojourn there. But chaste Joseph, with the insight of the pure of heart, recognized God's hand reaching from end to end mightily and ordering all things sweetly: "God sent me before you to preserve a remnant for you in the land, and to deliver you in a striking way. Not you but God sent me here" (Gen. 45:7f).

It was God, too, who brought the stay in Egypt to a close; His plans called for something better. He Himself took the initiative, wresting the poor sufferers from the grasp of Pharaoh and leading them out into the freedom of the desert.

The deliverance from Egypt had its sequel in the desert wandering and the conquest of Chanaan. The weary no-mads crossed the Jordan dry-shod, as previously they had passed unharmed through the parted waters of the Red Sea. The capture of Jericho and Hai followed in quick succession, and each conquest involved an act of God. All those with a heart to believe could see in these events a proof of present love and a pledge of future mercy.

Everything was from God—the people, the land, the lawgiver. So, too, Israel's first great prophet was a man of God's making. Samuel came as a gift of heaven to a barren mother, who recognized the Giver in His gift and made grateful return by consecrating to Him forever the boy He had bestowed. To many the miracle of Samuel's birth seemed a unique wonder of God's goodness. But for Anna, his mother, it was only one of many similar incidents, all proving that God is always at work to save the world He has made. She rises, then, from the thought of her child to contemplate the greater wonder of the universal salvation always at hand:

> My heart hath rejoiced in the Lord;
>   and my strength is exalted in my God . . .
>   because I rejoice in thy salvation. . . .

> The Lord maketh poor and maketh rich;
>   he humbleth and he exalteth.
> He raiseth up the needy from the dust,
>   and lifteth up the poor from the dust,
>   that he may sit with princes,
>   and hold the throne of glory.
>
> (1 Sam. 2:1, 7f.)

Whatever Israel was, whatever it had, all was God's work; He was always in the midst of His people to produce good things from nothing and to renew after failure.

The prophets saw this truth energizing the whole course of their nation's history. God had taken part in every incident from first to last:

> He found them in a wilderness,
>   a wasteland of howling desert.
> He shielded them and cared for them,
>   guarding them as the apple of His eye.
> As an eagle incites its nestlings forth
>   by hovering over its brood,
> So He spread His wings to receive them
>   and bore them up on His pinions.
> The Lord alone was their leader.
>
> (Deut: 32:10-12)

The prophet Ezechiel glimpsed the true picture with delicate sensitivity and painted it with the warm glow of consummate artistry. He saw a piteous babe, just born, cast upon the open field where it lay weltering in its blood. God passed by, and looked upon the poor little thing with love, and lavished upon it a devoted care that brought the child to rich and lovely maturity (Ez. 16).

But the time came when faithless Israel sickened and died; its dry bones littered the white sand and bleached under a blistering sun. Once more God intervened to save. Drawing together the scattered bones, He covered each skeleton with flesh and sinew, and breathed the gift of life into it: "The spirit came into them; they came alive and stood upright, a vast army" (37:10).

Thus it always was. God's creative power hovered over an earth that was "waste and void" to produce all that was fair and good. In return, He asked for one thing: let Israel live in constant awareness of her dependence upon Him. Time and again, therefore, He reminded His people of their need for Him. His is the sovereign will that rules the present; His is the wisdom that creates the future; His is the power that makes all reality. Whatever Israel was or might become, it owed all to the simple fact that God's loving gaze had rested upon it.

But it is easy for man to forget his benefactor and to despise what he has received. It was a chronic ailment for God's people. They tended to ignore the strong hand which upheld them; they seemed to resent their need for support.

The prophets struggled against this spirit of proud self-sufficiency. Sent by God to proclaim divine truth, they sought to dissolve the lie of Israel's self-reliance. Isaia, greatest of them all, dedicated his whole ministry to the laborious task of shifting attention from man to God. The vision he saw in the Temple inaugurated this mission. As he gazed on the Lord "seated on a high and lofty throne," he heard the angels sing, "Holy, holy, holy is the Lord of hosts" (6:1, 3). A sense of divine transcendence marked his soul with living awareness of his own frail creaturehood. Day after day he thundered against everything human which reared in pride before God. Fearlessly he sang his paeans of humility "against all that is proud and arrogant" (2:12).

But in the Temple Isaia also came to know in a new way the immanence of God. For he heard the angels sing, "All the earth is filled with His glory" (6:3); all that it contains is of His making. What comfort in these words! The land of Zabulon and Nephthali might be shrouded in darkness and torn by anguish; God would bring light and joy (9:1f). Israel would be reduced to a remnant and scattered to a distant nation; under God's lead, the remnant would return and, through His power, would once more become a mighty nation (10:20f). A charred stump might be the last vestige of a once verdant forest; but from it a divine shoot would grow (11:1). The God of power and mercy could produce anything from nothing, so long as men were sincere enough to acknowledge their need of Him and to "lean upon the Lord, the Holy One of Israel, in truth" (10:20). This assurance made Isaia an incorrigible optimist. "By waiting and by calm you shall be saved, in quiet and in trust your strength lies" (30:15).

His teaching explains the regular reappearance of human goodness in Israel's history. The holy men and women who take part in the story all bowed low before God with that total surrender which enabled Him to do great things for them. The later prophets call these blessed ones the *anawim*—"the humble and lowly people"; and they refer to their spirit as *anawah*—"lowliness." These words are suggestive tokens rather than complete titles, for no single word could ever contain a spirit so rich. At the same time, however, they are particularly apt terms, for they symbolize perfectly the Isaian formula for gaining God's favor.

Israel never attached special value to poverty, though it was always a reality in Israel. Poor people always existed in the land and the nation's early laws made prudent provision for their care. According to God's promises, the people had a right to comfort and security. Those who suffered want were considered unfortunate. Far from being something desirable, poverty was looked upon as a lack of the good things God had pledged.

The prophets, however, introduced a new note. The poverty of eighth-century Israel was due, not merely to misfortune, but also to criminal encroachments of the wealthy. In dealing with poverty, therefore, the prophets of the period—Amos and Osee, Isaia and Michea—confronted not only a social problem but also a moral abuse that continued through the following century down to the fall of Jerusalem. The prophets looked upon the poor as innocent victims of evil practice and cruel oppression; naturally, then, they spoke of them with new overtones of sympathy. In comparison with the fraudulent rich the poor are in the right, and their cause is just. God is on their side and they can lay claim to His special protection. But this does not mean that poverty itself becomes automatic holiness in His eyes. Jeremia considered the poor people of his day as reprehensible before God as the rich (5:4). Even more pointedly, the wisdom literature, written long after the prophets and in the light of their teaching, always spoke of poverty as an evil to avoid and, often, as evil in its cause.

But the prophets' use of the vocabulary of poverty was never forgotten. They had employed it freely in a religious context; they had spoken of the poor with sympathy and had represented their misery as crying out to God for mercy. Thus they prepared the way for the transformation of the vocabulary of poverty into a vocabulary of grace. The basis of this transfer is the Isaian principle that God works His divine effects only when man recognizes human insufficiency. The occasion for transfer is any personal experience of human powerlessness. The miseries of life and the inability of most men to cope with them, the vicissitudes of social struggle and the readiness of the strong to trample on the weak, the instability of man's will and the radical weakness of all things human: these trying and humbling experiences came frequently enough into the lives of God's friends to fill them with poignant awareness of their own poverty and constant need for His help. They must depend wholly upon Him and look to Him for everything or perish. What was more natural, then, than that they should speak to God with the very words that sounded on the lips of the poor? Often enough these holy ones were poor in reality; always they were poor in spirit.

Even the earliest heroes of Israel sought God's help as poor men. Wealthy Abraham assumed the posture and used the phrases of the mendicant when he pleaded with God for the saving of Sodom. So, too, a later writer sums up Moses' whole character with a single word that expresses his poverty of spirit: "Moses himself was by far the meekest man [*anaw*] on the face of the earth" (Num. 12:3). Holy Anna, pleading for a child, drew God's attention to her share in the misery of the poor: "O Lord of hosts, if thou wilt look down on the affliction [*ani*] of thy maidservant" (I Sam. 1:11). God's true friends felt themselves to be really poor before Him. Dependence and loving surrender were the breath of their life.

This spirit pulses in every page of the prophet Jeremia. He is the poor man par excellence, for no prophet equals him in piteous pleading for the help of God. By temperament his whole being was exquisitely sensitized to pain. A warmhearted, emotional man, he was keenly alive to love and could feel the opposition of others in every fibre of his soul. Yet God asked him to inveigh against all in

Israel. What a fearful vocation for a sensitive man! Poor
Jeremia always felt the heartache of this lifetime struggle,
and he cried out: "My grief is incurable, my heart within
me is faint" (8:18). He needed God in the way a suffering
poor man needs a friend to help him in his indigence and
to defend him against unjust oppression. The harassed
prophet, therefore, used the words of the poor to express
his misery and to plead for God's pity.

Once Jeremia had written his personal journal, others
also felt free to use his style in their intimate dealings with
God. But above all others, the authors of the Psalms were
truly kindred spirits. Causse has aptly named the Psalter
a "Book of the Poor," not because, as he suggests, it was
composed only by the party of the poor after the exile, but
because it is the outpouring of hearts that were steeped in
lowly dependence and total surrender. These authors belonged to no particular social class; one at least, King
David, must have been wealthy. But they were all conscious of need for God. A humbling sense of human powerlessness, mingled with strong trust in God, filled their souls
with readiness to serve, patience in waiting, and the clinging love of a child. All this is contained in the single word
anawah—poverty of spirit; it is the theme that pervades
the whole Psalter.

The Psalmists were friends of God. More than anything
they say, the very way they say it is proof of this. They
are so sure of God's love that, at times, they seem Prome-
thean in daring. Fearlessly they lay bare their whole soul
because they are certain God will understand. Whatever
misery drained them of strength, there was always one
thought to sustain them: God was their friend, He would
not abandon them. The author of Psalm 21 cried out:
"My God, my God, why have you forsaken me, far from

my prayer, from the words of my cry?" (v. 2). But because he was certain of God's friendship, he continued to plead insistently: "Be not far from me, for I am in distress; be near, for I have no one to help me. . . . But you, O Lord, be not far from me" (vv. 12, 20). So, too, the author of Psalm 68 was "sunk in the abysmal swamp where there is no foothold" (v. 3); but he knew that he could always count on his divine friend: "Answer me, O Lord, for bounteous is your kindness; in your great mercy turn toward me. Hide not your face from your servant" (v. 17 f.).

These men needed such confidence, for time and again they were stripped of all human support and felt the full powerlessness of creaturehood. Tasting anguish within and suffering oppression from without, cut off from friends and cruelly betrayed, they tasted the nauseating dregs of human weakness. No heartsick existentialist has experienced a deeper distrust of all things created than the authors of Psalms 9B, 21, 54, 55, and many others.

God was their only savior. No matter what their need, the Psalmist could always count on Him to intervene. How or when or where they did not know; but His was the wisdom and power and love, and so in His own good time all would come well.

This attitude of soul was bound to influence the true Israelite in his dealings with others. The inward spirit of *anawah,* the habit of looking away from men to God, permeated even his exterior actions with the fragrance of peace. The tranquillity of complete dependence upon God overflowed in a spirit of meekness and humility. Others might take advantage of him, or mistreat and even persecute him; human help might collapse and trusted friends turn traitor. The psalms abound in descriptions of what God's holy ones had to endure. Yet always there was the

attitude of acceptance which marks the inveterately poor.
Though the Psalmist pleaded with God to intervene, he
always maintained the silent and calm forbearance of an
afflicted poor man who is certain his powerful protector
will soon put in an appearance. To have acted otherwise
would have been a lack of trust. Outer life flowed directly
from the heart. Rooted distrust of self and unfailing confidence in God radiated the outward tranquillity of meekness.

This was the spirit that God looked for in His people,
a spirit that found analogy in the experiences of the poor.
For the only attitude that rings true to man's creaturehood
is that which compounds a sense of personal powerlessness
with unfailing confidence in the power of God and total
surrender to the guidance of His will.

When the Isaian principle of dependence had transformed the vocabulary of poverty, the prophets following
the exile called this spirit *anawah*—poverty—and those
who possessed it the *anawim*—the poor. Whereas Amos
in the eighth century told his people; "Seek good and not
evil that you may live" (5:14). Sophonia in the sixth century uses the new vocabulary to make the recommendation
more pointed: "Seek the Lord, all you humble [*anawim*]
of the earth, who have observed his law. Seek justice,
seek humility [*anawah*]" (2:3). The later prophets saw
clearly that goodness becomes real through poverty of
heart. So, too, the author of the last chapters of the prophecy of Isaia teaches that this spirit alone could win favor
from the Lord; for in his pages God's word bears the message: "This is the one whom I approve; the lowly and
afflicted man who trembles at my word" (66:2).

It was natural, then, for the late prophets to identify the
blessed remnant of the future as a group of *anawim*. These

holy men and women, so dear to God, were to stand on the threshold of the new age to greet the Messiah and to enter with Him into the new kingdom. All that was best in Israel's heritage must be vital reality in their souls. Above all else, therefore, they must possess that spiritual poverty which alone rings true in man's dealings with God. Sophonia was the first to state this explicitly; for it is in his prophecy that God promises: "I will leave as a remnant in your midst a people *humble and lowly,* who shall take refuge in the name of the Lord" (3:12). Later, in the last chapter of Isaia, the Messiah pledges His mission of mercy to this group: "The Spirit of the Lord God is upon me, because the Lord has anointed me. He has sent me to bring glad tidings to the lowly [*anawim*], to heal the brokenhearted, . . . to comfort all who mourn" (61:1-2). Indeed, the Messiah Himself would be characterized by this beautiful spirit of the *anawim;* He too would be meek and humble of heart. For just before the light of prophecy dimmed in Israel, Zacharia beheld the future king and sketched this portrait of Him: "See, your king shall come to you; a just savior is he, meek [*ani*] and riding on an ass" (9:9).

All this came to pass.

When at last He appeared, the humble Christ, those who came forward to greet Him were the truly poor in spirit— Joseph, Zachary and Elizabeth, Simeon and Ann, the Shepherds and the Magi; these formed His court, the holy remnant promised by the prophets. But long before, His gaze had rested with special love on Mary, the young Jewess of Nazareth. No other was so truly poor in spirit, so keenly conscious of need for Him, so perfectly surrendered to His will. That is why He chose her to be His mother—the most humble of the *anawim.*

When the angel brought her God's message and asked her to become the mother of His son, Mary accepted the divine will with total surrender: "Behold the handmaid of the Lord; be it done to me according to thy word" (Luke 1:38). This humble acceptance opened her heart to receive the greatest of God's gifts, His own Son. Ever after, it was always the same; her spirit of *anawah* was the secret of all His favors to her. She herself knew this, for when Elizabeth congratulated her on the peerless privilege of her maternity, Mary answered with the voice of the *anawim*. For in her Magnificat we hear mingled strains from the song of Miriam and the canticle of Anna and the prayer of Judith:

> My soul magnifies the Lord,
>   and my spirit rejoices in God my Savior;
> Because He has regarded the lowliness
>   of his handmaid; . . .
> Because He who is mighty has done great things for me,
>   and holy is His name. . . .
> He has shown might with His arm,
>   He has scattered the proud in the conceit of their heart.
> He has put down the mighty from their thrones,
>   and has exalted the lowly.
> He has filled the hungry with good things,
>   and the rich He has sent away empty.
> He has given help to Israel, His servant,
>   mindful of His mercy.
>
> (Luke 1:46-54)

All her life long Mary grew ever more dear to God by growing ceaselessly in the spirit of the *anawim*. May we not say of her what the Epistle to the Hebrews said of her Son: she learned *anawah* from the things that she suffered (*cf.,* Heb. 5:8). Everything which God permitted to hap-

pen in her life served only to deepen the dependence and
to enrich the surrender contained in the first word she
uttered: "Behold thy handmaid. Be it done to me according to thy word." Always, too, this growth in inward life
radiated a greater loveliness upon her whole external bearing. Within and without, Mary was the fairest of the
anawim.

Time and again she had to wait on God, certain of His
will and power to help but quite in the dark as to when
and where. She had to wait on Him when she felt Joseph's
wonderment about her pregnancy and sensed the problem
that lay heavy upon his mind. She was certain that in
God's good time all would come well, but for the moment
it meant keen suffering and inviolable silence—and quiet
surrender.

Even more she had to endure the anguish which goes
deepest into the heart because it touches someone who is
dearer than life itself. For instance, there was the day she
entered the Temple court to present her little one to His
Father. An aged man took Him from her arms and, with
eyes aglow, uttered words that pierced her soul: "Behold,
this child is destined for the fall and for the rise of many
in Israel, and for a sign that shall be contradicted" (Luke
2:34). Again, the hour struck when loss snatched Him
out of her life. It was a very "poor" mother who sought
Him sorrowing; for that day her soul agonized with the
awareness that everything precious had slipped from her
grasp. She knew, of course, that in due time all would
be well; but all the same the days of search were shrouded
in blackness. That is why her "fiat" in those dark hours
filled her soul as never before with the surrender of the
anawim.

If anything, all her Son's recorded words to her served

the one great purpose of deepening this spirit within her. His every sentence steadied her gaze on the will of the Father. Thus when she found Him in the Temple, He reminded her that the "Father's business" must always come first" (Luke 2:49). When she asked Him for the courtesy of turning water into wine for the embarrassed hosts at Cana, He called her attention to the fact that the hour which the Father had assigned had not yet come (Jn. 2:4). Only then did He work the wonder. Later, people spoke to Him of His mother and of the bond between Him and her (Luke 11:27f; Mt. 12:46-50). But both times He made clear that what counted most was the tie that united them in the spirit of the *anawim*—perfect fidelity to the will of the Father.

She needed this spirit in its fullness; for, in God's eternal plan, she was to come closer to Him than any other through the most perfect of all surrenders. "Now there was standing by the cross of Jesus His mother. . . . When Jesus, therefore, saw His mother and the disciple standing by, whom He loved, He said to His mother, 'Woman, behold thy son' " (Jn. 19: 25 f.). Never before or after has God asked any creature for such complete detachment from everything human and for such total surrender to His will. In place of Jesus she was asked to accept John; for Him who is all, the disciple who was only a man. At the beginning of everything, Mary, the Queen of the *anawim,* uttered the perfect word He was waiting for: "Behold the handmaid of the Lord; be it done to me according to thy word."

At every moment she met Him with the full-hearted surrender which is the very essence of the spirit of *anawah*. This is what He asks of all His followers—the spirit that formed the holiness of the Old Testament saints, that inspired the beautiful prayers of the Psalter, and figured so largely in the prophets' dreams for the future. On the day, therefore, when He first drew a blueprint of the ideal Christian character, He sketched with deft strokes the features of the *anawim*:

> Blessed are the poor in spirit. . . .
> Blessed are the meek. . . .
> Blessed are they who mourn. . . .
> Blessed are they who hunger and thirst for justice. . . .
> Blessed are the merciful. . . .
> Blessed are the pure of heart. . . .
> Blessed are the peacemakers. . . .
> Blessed are they who suffer persecution
>   for justice's sake. . .
>
> (Mt. 5:3-10).

Perhaps, as He spoke these words, He was recalling verses from the Psalms or from the prophets.

But there is a simpler likelihood. All He had to do was to think of His mother in the poor home at Nazareth and to put into words the beautiful spirit He saw in her—the lowliest and the loveliest of the *anawim*.

CHAPTER 4   NEW LIGHT

ON THE GOSPELS

In 1920, at the close of the first World War, the German scholars Rudolph Bultmann, Martin Dibelius, Karl Schmidt and others worked concurrently though not in concert to open the Gospels to agnostics dominated by Heideggerian philosophy. As zealous army chaplains, these students of the Bible had come into contact with soldiers whose philosophy denied all divine intervention in the world of men. Working within the same philosophic framework, Bultmann and the others devised a means to make the Gospels meaningful to men who could not envision the supernatural.

The new approach viewed the Gospels as the fabrication of the primitive Christian community. "Community" became the password for full access to the Christian message. Whatever riches the Gospels contain derived, form and substance, from the creative activity of a community which had come to believe that Jesus had risen from the dead. This faith created a message about Christ for the sole purpose of helping man achieve authentic understand-

ing of himself before God. Here the center of gravity was
not the past but the present; the point of interest was not
the Jesus of history who was almost unknown, but the
Christ of faith whose words and deeds were created to meet
every human need.

This thesis was offered as an outcome of Gospel analysis.
Following the method which Hermann Gunkel had used
in the Old Testament these scholars studied the Gospels
not as unified works of a literary author but as a mere
collection of individual units. One by one these units were
subjected to careful analysis on the supposition that the
form of each would reveal the sociological factor which
brought the unit into being. This method, called form
criticism, regarded each unit as the product of a need in
community life. Preaching, liturgy, controversy — these
factors were looked upon as the creative agents of the
Gospel forms.

From the very beginning other scholars like Charles
Dodd and T. W. Manson reacted strongly against the postulates of German form criticism. While acknowledging
that large portions of the Gospels were first formulated
in the teaching apostolate of the Church, they denied cate-
gorically that the community had created these elements.
A community creates nothing; it is rather the womb in
which the compelling thought of an original genius becomes viable. They pointed out, moreover, that no one
in the community could qualify as the originator of a Gospel message which contradicted cardinal tenets of Judaism
and ran counter to prevalent Jewish hopes.

Gradually even the disciples of the form critics came
to share this adverse reaction. They sensed the embarrassment of Bultmann when he was asked to explain the enigma

of a nameless community creating within twenty years a fully formed Christianity without basis in fact. The theory of a definitive Christian Gospel coming to life in so short a time lacks a *raison d'être* if it rests on the obscure figure of a merely human Jesus and on a life without challenge or meaning. The first Christian community was made up of ignorant and hardheaded Jews who would have been the last ones to turn Jesus into a "Son of God." They themselves had lived through the events of His public life like the others to whom they preached. Eyewitnesses are not duped by a hoax when they have everything to lose.

Under pressure of this reaction the pendulum has swung away from the thesis of form criticism. At the end of the second World War another school arose which shifted attention away from the study of individual units in the Gospels to concentrate on the Gospels as unified compositions of literary authors. This school of redaction criticism is represented by scholars like Gunther Bornkamm, Hans Conzelmann, and Willi Marxsen.

It is the Evangelist who has now become the focal point of interest. His literary activity, his theological insights and purpose, his background of personal interests have left a distinctive mark on his literary work. Each Evangelist contributed so much to his own presentation of the Gospel message that Willi Marxsen has written: "There are no Synoptic Gospels." The day of the *Diatesseron* is gone forever; the Gospels can no longer be lumped together. Each must be studied as the unique work of a literary artist.

The recognition of a unique literary quality in each Gospel is not new. Père Lagrange, for instance, in the masterful introductions to his commentaries studied carefully the special contribution of each Evangelist. He was fully aware that the sacred author has forged a message in the fire of his own spirit. The text inspired by God involved also a full play of human powers.

The recent emphasis on this aspect is blighted by a certain weakness. The school of redaction criticism gives the impression at times that it has merely shifted creativity from the "community" of the form criticism school to the "evangelist" of its own school. A reader of Hans Conzelmann's *Theology of St. Luke* will find himself asking, "Is so large a part of the Gospel merely the creation of Luke?"

Weakness as well as strength characterize the approach both of form criticism and redaction criticism. Biblists of these schools center attention on factors which must be taken into account if the Gospels are to be studied in the spirit in which they were written. Both schools, however, have tendencies which must be corrected if true perspectives are to be maintained. These perspectives, however, have been greatly sharpened by the work of the past forty years. Gospel study today occupies a vantage point gained by the positive advances of form and redaction critics.

Previously Gospel study was bi-dimensional. The reader moved from his analysis of the text to the level of the actual words and deeds of Jesus. This procedure rested on the presumption that the Gospels offer a consecutive biography of Christ, a stenographic report of His words and a chronological record of His deeds. Viewing the Gospels in this light men wrote lives of Christ in the same style as modern biographies.

A certain malaise was inevitable. Authors like Lagrange and Lebreton, Fillion and Prat seemed uncertain in their reconstructions. It had to be so. The conflicting reports of the different Evangelists, the notable lacunae in their accounts, the divergent geography and time computation which set one Evangelist against another—elements like these called for constant harmonization. The simple fact is that the Evangelists never intended to provide material for a biography in the modern sense of the word.

Their story of Christ centers in the words and deeds of Jesus of Nazareth; but this portrait of Him reveals a "likeness" rather than an "image"; it is an inspired interpretation of what He really was rather than a photographic reproduction of what He seemed to be. The Evangelists present His life as illumined by the revealing light of the Spirit who, after Pentecost, recalled to the mind of the Church all that He had said and done, in order to make known the profound meaning of His words and the eternal import of His deeds.

This intermediary level of the Church's understanding of Christ is essential for full understanding of the Gospel. Something is missing if Gospel study is merely bi-dimensional. Between the inspired text and the actual life of Jesus there intervened thirty years of the Church's teaching. All three levels must be kept in mind if we are to glimpse the luminous Gospel portrait of the Son of God.

The first level is that of the inspired text itself. Each Evangelist as a literary artist has drawn his own portrait of Christ. Native gifts of style and personal theological interests formed the mold into which he cast his materials. Even when using common sources each Evangelist reshapes the data to accord with his own equipment as writer and thinker.

Mark burned with desire to show that Jesus was the Christ even though men did not receive Him. He reiterates this theme; he heaps up evidence to prove a plus quality in everything Jesus said or did: "Who then is this, that even the wind and the sea obey Him?" (Mk. 4:40). Mark achieves this portrayal of the divine Christ by dividing his Gospel into two neat parts, each rising climactically to a resounding cry of faith. The first half of his Gospel (ch. 1-8) culminates in the confession of Peter the Jew, "Thou art the Christ" (Mk. 8:29). The second half (ch. 8-15) rises to the awe-filled cry of the gentile centurion on Calvary, "Truly this man was the Son of God!" (Mk. 15-39).

Mark, however, was hampered by literary shortcomings. His style is pedestrian and repetitious like that of a beginner. He therefore followed the easier course and incorporated source material without retouching it. If his Gospel is vital and colorful it is because he has reproduced exactly the memoirs of Peter. This dependence on his sources brings the Gospel of Mark close to the bedrock of tradition. The Christ of Mark is strikingly human in the play of his emotions, in the earthy color of His deeds, and in the limitation of even His miraculous powers.

Christ in Mark is a study of chiaroscuro, truly divine yet wholly human. This development is only one of many distinctive features in this Gospel. To share the full light of Mark's unique vision we must study the mystery of Jesus from his perspective. Full familiarity with his style and purpose, clear knowledge of his plan, painstaking analysis of his Gospel as a personal literary composition—all this is essential if we are to garner full riches on this first level of Gospel study, the inspired text.

Luke, Matthew, and John also present their own distinctive portrait of Christ. "Mark," writes Père Lagrange, "works in the warm earthiness of terra cotta; Luke sculptures from white marble." For Luke, both in the Gospel and in Acts, geography is theological; his mind is fascinated by the vast sweep of Christianity's universal mission, from humble beginnings in Jerusalem to glorious consummation in Rome. Matthew's outlook is colored by a strong interest in ecclesiology; his style is often hieratic and liturgical. John, on the other hand, is a sacramentalist with a mystic's insight into the mystery of the Word inspiriting flesh.

This interpretative activity of the Evangelists has long been recognized. Previously, however, the next move was to proceed from the Gospel text to the actual words and deeds of Jesus. Recent form-criticism studies have now focused light on an intervening level: the community. This intermediary stage has always been well known to Catholics. We above all others have constantly affirmed that the Gospel was first lived and preached before it was written. Today we must face the implications of this thesis.

Whatever the Evangelists wrote they had to receive from the Church, for none except John were eyewitnesses of the ministry of Christ. Mark entered on the scene only after the Resurrection; Luke was a gentile doctor from Antioch; the canonical "Matthew" was an anonymous author of the late first century. These synoptic Evangelists had to draw on materials which only the Church could supply. John, too, was markedly dependent on the full faith of the Church, for he wrote not a mere reproduction of words and deeds but a profound interpretation of their meaning and mystery.

This dependence of the Evangelists upon the Church focuses light on a second level in Gospel study. The materials which the Evangelists record were already illumined by the full light of the Spirit.

The Church has never locked up her memories of Jesus in a hermetically sealed box to be opened only when someone wanted to write a documented history, with barren references to exact times and places, with sterile photographic reproductions. On the contrary, she constantly interpreted and applied the words and deeds of Jesus that they might play a vital and informative role in her own life. The history of the Man-God was never viewed as a mere incident of the past; it was seen rather as a power always operative, ringing a challenge and charting a course for Christians in the present.

This daily use of His words and deeds was bound to shape their telling and to bring out what was deep and rich in every event. The Gospel record, therefore, drawing its material from the Church, often shows an identification tag of community usage.

The miracle stories, for instance, are drawn from the preaching of the apostles. This preaching involved the recital of how Jesus "went about doing good and healing all who were in the power of the devil" (Acts 10:38). Keeping to the demands of oral style and following the rabbinical pattern, the first preachers described the wonders of Christ with careful economy of phrase and with indifference to irrelevant details of time, place, and circumstance. The account was whittled down to brief notes on three phases: (1) the illness and condition of the sufferer; (2) the action of Christ the wonder-worker; (3) the saving effect of His power.

The Gospel miracle stories reflect this community use. They are not a candid photo with background and details but a clean etching of what is strictly essential. The story of the cure of Peter's mother-in-law is typical; it presents only the three points listed above and nothing more: (1) a brief indication of her illness—"Simon's mother-in-law was keeping her bed, sick with a fever" (Mk. 1:30); (2) a terse action photo of what the miracle worker did: "Drawing near, he took her by the hand and raised her up"

(v. 31); (3) a cryptic final statement of the effect: "The fever left her at once" (v. 31).

This crisp brevity is explained by Mark's dependence on a previous oral form which centered all attention on Christ's saving action. Details which would be essential for integrating this incident into a biography of Christ have all been omitted. Such poverty of detail and concentration on what is essential characterize most of the Gospel miracle stories.

The community had also a liturgy to prepare for its distinctive rites of Baptism and the "breaking of bread." It was natural to incorporate into the liturgy the story of those events in Jesus' life which prepared for the sacraments of the Church or provided a parallel to them. The recountal of these incidents in the liturgical assembly called for a hieratic style and the rhythm of solemnity.

When incorporated into the written Gospels these readings of the liturgical assembly retain the color and tone of their cultic origin. The description of the Last Supper in the Synoptics is typical. The courses of food, the songs, the conversation—all this is omitted. We find nothing but a sharply etched portrayal of Christ's eucharistic action in a style which is solemn and lapidary.

The early Church had also to answer many questions and to solve bristling problems. As each difficulty arose, memories of Jesus were rekindled and relevant words of His were recounted. There would have been the question about divorce. Was the Church to use the concession granted by Moses? If so, was she to follow the lenient casuistry of the rabbi Hillel or adopt the stern requirements of the rabbi Shammai? The remembrance of a pointed word of Christ ended the whole discussion: "Whoever puts away his wife and marries another commits adultery"

(Mk. 10:11). This saying became a directive principle in the community and as such was incorporated into the Gospel.

Other problems called for solution. What was to be done with gentiles who wished to enter the Church? (Cf. Acts 10:15.) Some urged that they first become Jews. It was helpful to recall how Jesus had dealt with gentiles. In healing the servant of a gentile centurion He offered to enter the gentile's house even though Jews looked upon this as a defilement. What is more, He gave full praise to the man's peerless faith: "Amen, I have not found so great a faith in Israel" (Mt. 8:10). This conduct of Christ directed the Church's attitude towards gentile converts; she accepted them just as they were. This incident lived in the Church's memory; more than likely it was already in writing when the Evangelists inserted it into their Gospels.

The early Church had its conflicts with a hard core of Jewish Christians who wanted to couple observance of the Law with the service of Christ. It was encouraging to remember that Jesus had faced similar controversies. His solution of these thorny problems provided ammunition in controversies which the Church herself had to conduct. The frequent rehearsal of His conflicts resulted in a clearly defined literary form which we today call the pronouncement story. The pattern is easy to detect in the Gospels. Everything in the narrative is pared down to bare essentials in order to place emphasis on the conclusive pronouncement of Jesus.

The story in Luke 5:29-32 provides an apt illustration. First a single sentence describes the situation: "There was a great gathering of publicans and others who were at table with them" (v. 29). Next follows the criticism not only as

Jesus heard it from the Pharisees but also as the first Christians heard it from their critics: "Why do you eat and drink with publicans and sinners?" (v. 30). This criticism is met with a memorable pronouncement of Jesus which would serve as a principle of action for the whole Church: "It is not the healthy who need a physician, but they who are sick. I have not come to call the just, but sinners to repentance" (vv. 31-32).

This was the kind of material which the Evangelists had to use in their account of Jesus' ministry. The majority of words and events in our Gospels are there not only because they figured in the life of Christ but also because they served some vital need in the life of the early Church.

It is unwarranted, therefore, to look upon the Gospels as a journalist's report of what happened yesterday. Whatever memories of Christ they contain lived a fruitful life in the soil of the community. The narratives, therefore, do not follow a chronological succession of events; they do not guarantee verbatim quotations of Jesus' words. The very formulas which the Gospels should have treasured in exact reproduction (e.g., the Lord's prayer, the words of eucharistic consecration) are found in as many different forms as there are Evangelists who recount them.

What the Evangelists have preserved for us is not a photographic reproduction of the words and deeds of Jesus but an interpretative portrait as the Church herself prepared it under the light of the Holy Spirit. Jesus Himself had promised, "The Holy Spirit . . . will teach you all things, and bring to your mind whatever I have said to you" (Jn. 14:26). Under the light of this Spirit both the Evangelist and the Church came to see not only what Jesus said and did but, far better, what He really meant.

It is only a study of the Gospels from these two levels

of the inspired Evangelist and the Spirit-guided Church that
brings full understanding of the third level on which all
else is based. This is the historical level of the earthly life
of Jesus, His words and deeds. A casual reader of the
Gospel text might see in His miracles merely human benef-
icence restoring health to the body. When seen, however, through the eyes of the Church and of the Evangelist
these miracles reveal the saving power of the messianic
Son of God.

We ourselves know what "to hear" means in the rite
of Baptism and in the story of the cure of the deaf and
dumb man. In the light of the Church's application of
this miracle to the transformation of the soul the story
comes alive with new meaning. The miracle is now seen
as more than mere restoration of speech and hearing.
Working as the Messiah, Jesus changed the whole man,
giving not only physical hearing but also spiritual power
to hear the word of God, bestowing not only physical
speech but also spiritual power to speak the praises of
God. The Church's use of the miracle story in her liturgy
brings us to share her own deep understanding of the full
meaning of every messianic miracle.

In the same way the agony in the garden gains new
significance when one remembers that it was originally
part of the primitive catechesis. The Greek words which
the Church employed and the Evangelists repeated bear
the imprint of community use, echoing words frequently
repeated in early catechetical instructions: "Watch and
pray." "Pray lest you enter into temptation." These were
the words with which the first preachers urged their converts to bear trial and to endure struggle as a real share
in the messianic tribulation which must precede the glorious *parousia*.

In the light of the contribution which each Christian must make in "prayer and watchfulness," the Church was able to interpret the true meaning of Jesus' words to His Apostles in the garden. His plea, "Watch with me," was not an appeal for human sympathy. It was rather the heartful cry of a father and shepherd urging His own to be faithful to God in the dread "hour" of messianic struggle with the powers of darkness.

Through this interpretation coming from the first days of the Church and preserved for us in the Gospel's Greek translation of Jesus' Aramaic words, the scene in the garden comes alive with deep meaning which rings resonantly in the heart of every reader. The Apostle in the garden and the Christian in the struggle of daily life are one. Both hear the same plea to "watch and pray" that they may be found worthy of the "hour" of Christ's supreme glory.

Gospel study, therefore, means work on three levels. It is only when we view its message from the perspectives of the Evangelist's insight and the Church's understanding that we too, under the light of the Holy Spirit, shall come to appreciate the full, rich meaning of Christ's words and deeds during the days of His earthly life.

An example may help to make all this clear. The floor of the ocean is littered with sea shells. Only some of these are swept onto the shore. There wind and rain smooth away sharp edges. The sunlight brings out rich coloring. A man finds them there, gathers them up and forms them into a vase, beautiful in shape and color. To appreciate the exquisite beauty of the vase we not only gaze at its whole contour and color-pattern but we study also the graceful turn and delicate tint of every shell.

It is the same with the Gospels. Our Lord's life was like an ocean bed filled with words and deeds in such abundance that books could not contain them. Only some of these reached the shore of the primitive community. There the wind and light of the Spirit shaped the telling of each deed and illumined its deep meaning. The Evangelists gathered together these living memories and molded them into a Gospel under the light of the Spirit. No two Gospels are the same; each has its own contour and coloring.

To measure the truth and to appreciate the beauty of the Gospel we cannot be content to study merely the formative work of the Evangelist and the over-all impression of his literary composition. We must also study each unit in the Gospel, as we would study each shell in a vase, to discover what the Holy Spirit disclosed to the Church— the full meaning of each event and the vital significance of each word in the life of Jesus.

CHAPTER 5

THE POWER
OF HIS
RESURRECTION

DEVOTION to the sacred passion of Jesus Christ, as we know it today, is a gift which comes to us from the piety of the Middle Ages. In the early Church the thought of imitating Christ in His sufferings, the idea of meditating and preaching on the Passion was comparatively unknown. The Passion was then looked upon as the "Passio beata," or, the "Blessed Passion."

The early Church Fathers reveal a spirit and a mentality very close to the Gospel of St. John. In John, divinity radiates through every moment of our Lord's life. John sees our Lord suffused with glory from the very beginning, so that the Passion story in John glows with exultation. In John, the "lifting up" is not merely the lifting up in the bitter suffering of the Passion; it is the lifting up in the glorious Resurrection and Ascension. He sees the cross as already fully alight with the glory which was to follow upon it. He does not draw a distinction between the moments before and the moments after.

It was only in the Middle Ages with the piety of the

Cistercian school, exemplified in women like St. Gertrude and St. Mechtild, in men like St. Bernard and above all St. Francis of Assisi, that the great principles of the spiritual life are applied to the details of the Passion itself. It was certainly an authentic development in the thought of the Church, and there has followed from it much fruitful meditation and effective preaching.

We know, however, that preaching has at times deviated and that meditation on the passion of Christ has occasionally been more influenced by the psychology of masochism than by the truth of faith. And thus it is imperative that we be fully conscious of the principles of apostolic Christianity, so that preaching and meditation on the Passion be really life-giving.

St. Paul himself was not at all concerned with the details of the Passion. He tells us clearly in Corinthians: "We know no one according to the flesh. And even though we have known Christ according to the flesh [the details of his earthly life], yet now we know him so no longer. . . . In Christ . . . [all things] are made new" (2 Cor. 5:16f).

In St. Paul's epistles you will find only seven allusions to the details of the passion of Christ, and each time it is merely a casual allusion. "Jesus on the night before he died, was betrayed . . . ." Nothing more; no delay over what we would call the imitative qualities of the passion of Christ; no effort at setting up a psychological apparatus, as did St. Ignatius in the Spiritual Exercises, to bring us to imitate Christ's passion.

It is really only in the Epistle to the Hebrews—which Paul did not personally write—and likewise in the epistles of St. Peter, that we are urged to walk in the footsteps of Him who suffered. At the same time, however, in what St. Paul has given us, and in what we find in the *depositum*, there are principles which validate our own method of approach. It would be well to investigate these principles so that our own meditation and our own preaching can become more fruitful.

In the early Church it was not the Passion but the Resurrection which was to the fore. In the apostolic Church the Resurrection dominates all thinking.

In the early sermons in Acts, the focal point of the Apostles' preaching was the definitive salvation event of Christ's resurrection. This insight came to the Apostles at Pentecost. Our Blessed Lord and His life are a bridge between the world of the Old Testament and the world of the Church. That is why St. Mark begins his Gospel with the words, "This is the beginning of the Gospel of Jesus Christ, the Son of God." It is not the consummation. The earthly life described in the Gospel of Mark is the beginning of the Gospel which began at Pentecost.

Pope Pius XII expressed this thought very beautifully in *Mystici Corporis*: the Church he wrote, has come from the rib and the side of Christ on the cross. The Church is the creation of the Resurrection. Christ's work was to save and to redeem, to create the Church; the Church begins at the moment that Christ passes to His Father in newness of life.

Thus, the event of Pentecost was what we might call the "created act" of the Church. At that moment for the first time the Apostles came to know with the full light of the Spirit that this Jesus with whom they had lived, who had suffered and died, who had spoken with them in the forty days between the Resurrection and the Ascension, was in very truth the Yahweh of the Old Testament.

At Pentecost for the first time, the full light of the Spirit burst upon them. And what was the result? They simply became "drunk" with overpowering joy. They went through what mystical writers call "spiritual inebriation." It was an experience very much like that of St. Philip Neri, for instance, unable to go on at the altar because he was, as it were, intoxicated with the graces that were pouring into him; like that of St. John of the Cross going down the corridor, beating the wall with his hands lest he be swept away with prayer.

That is what the Apostles went through at Pentecost when there burst upon them for the first time this tremendous conviction that Jesus is really and truly Yahweh.

At that moment, therefore, the Apostles were confirmed in grace. Their conviction was so blinding that never again could they turn from Him. Not only that, but at that moment there was given to them the *parresia* (bold, courageous liberty) which was going to feature so largely in the Acts of the Apostles and in the epistles of St. Paul.

They go out now, men fluent with speech; men who were "all words," men who could not contain their message, men who might speak in broken Greek but men through whom this conviction would simply *pour* itself out even though they had to stutter and stammer it!

Our text translates this determination variously: "They spoke with courage . . . they spoke with confidence . . . they spoke with fearlessness." Always in the Greek text it is this same *parresia*.

At the moment of Pentecost their convictions were so burning that they "went out," as the Scripture will say again and again, "as witnesses of the Resurrection." They were not witnesses in the sense that they were giving apologetic argument that He had risen from the dead. That is not what the Resurrection meant to them. To them, it meant that this Jesus was the living *Kyrios,* and that here and now they were in dynamic contact with Him. Everywhere they went, they preached a "living Christ." He was the Kyrios; He was the Kingly Lord. And He had become that at the moment of His resurrection.

This Resurrection was not resuscitation. Jairus' daughter had been resuscitated—only to die again. Lazarus was resuscitated—only to die again.

The resurrection of Christ was, above all, a theological mystery. Jesus had certainly resuscitated as a man, but He had resuscitated as a man whose whole humanity was instinct with the very being of God. For the apostles the Resurrection meant that Jesus had risen from the dead— now no longer trammeled by the limitations of human life, but now a man whose divinity could function dynamically through His humanity.

That functioning of the divinity meant that this Jesus who was man could do what only God could do: He could give the Spirit which the Old Testament promised as the messianic gift par excellence. As the Father could give the creative Spirit, the illumining Spirit, the guiding Spirit, so now, this man as no one before could give the Spirit.

In his sermon at Pentecost St. Peter recounts what God has done for His people through Jesus in the days of His earthly life. "Men of Israel," he says, "hear these words. Jesus of Nazareth was a man approved by God among you by miracles and wonders and signs, which God did through him in the midst of you, as you yourselves know" (Acts 2:22). He quickly mentions the fact that He had been put to death.

He then announces: "For neither was he abandoned to hell, nor did his flesh see corruption. This Jesus God has raised up, and we are all witnesses of it. Therefore," and here we encounter the theological meaning of the Resurrection, "exalted by the right hand of God, and receiving from the Father the promise of the Holy Spirit, he had poured forth this Spirit which you see and hear."

"Let all the house of Israel know most assuredly," he concludes, "that God has made both Lord and Christ, this Jesus whom you crucified" (Acts 2:31-36). In our language today that is pure Adoptionism. To us who follow Chalcedon, Jesus was God from the moment of His Incarnation and all through His earthly life; He was always the Lord. But to the early Church this Jesus "God hath made Lord and Christ through His resurrection."

This thought is expressed even more strikingly by St. Paul at Antioch. After rehearsing all the dynamic interventions of God in the Old Testament, he shows that this salvific activity of God has come to its comsummation in what God has done to His Son Jesus. "So now," he says, "we bring you the good news that the promise made to our fathers God has fulfilled to us, their children, in raising up Jesus, as also it is written in the second Psalm, 'Thou art my son, this day have I begotten thee'" (Acts 13:32f).

But God begot Him from all eternity! Jesus was God in the moment of His Incarnation. And yet Paul seizes upon this phrase and sees His "begetting" at the moment of the Resurrection.

Language such as this belongs to the pre-theological stage of apostolic days. St. Paul does not investigate the nature of God. He is concerned with the simple fact that during the days of His earthly life Our Lord was man; He was bound by human limitations, by space, by time, by weakness; affected by human emotions, subject to the inclemencies of the weather, subject to fatigue, subject to sorrows, subject to depression, subject to a sense of frustration—subject to all these things, man through and through. That is the way He appeared.

Suddenly there is a transcendent change; this same man is now functioning divinely as Yahweh. At the moment of the Resurrection a tremendous change has come; for God then constituted this man "His messianic Son." This mode of presentation comes from a Hebrew mind, steeped in Old Testament thought-patterns.

Indeed, in an early credal formulary of the Roman Church, this same note of Adoptionism seems discernible to us who follow upon Chalcedon. St. Paul, possibly in order to gain the good favor of the Romans, opens his epistle by incorporating verbatim a formulary which they were using to express their faith.

My Gospel, he says, centers in the Son of God, "who was born to him according to the flesh" (The Greek word for "flesh" denotes "weak humanness,") born in his *weak humanness,* "a son of David, but who was manifested Son of God with power . . . through his resurrection" (Rom. 1:3f).

When we think of the phrase "son of God," we think of it in the static thought-categories of the Greeks; we think of it as referring to the nature as distinct from the activity. Not so with the Hebrews. When they speak of "the son of God" and refer to Jesus as the Son of God, made so by His resurrection, they think of this dynamic functioning of divinity in Jesus.

That truth of divinity manifested by the Resurrection dominates the thought of the early Church and the preaching of the Apostles. Wherever they went they preached that this Jesus, risen from the dead, was really and truly living, Yahweh Himself. People, therefore, were asked to accept Him, to believe in Him, and, believing in Him, to wait for His glorious return at the Parousia.

Obviously, in such preaching there was little room for the Passion. The early sermons in Acts which reflect authentically the thinking and the teaching of the Church, generally treated the Passion as something to apologize for. It was a problem and a very serious one at that, because pre-Christian Judaism knew nothing of a suffering Messiah. The beautiful themes about the Servant of Yahweh, in Isaia, chapters 42 and 49, 51 and 53; the renewal of that theme in chapter 12 of Zacharia, its intimation in Psalms like 21 and 68—those themes were never focused upon the Messiah but were applied to the entire messianic people.

And so it is, for instance, that the inter-Testamental literature in the period before Christ's coming reveals no appreciation of the fact that when the Messiah came he would suffer. The Psalms of Solomon; the Book of Enoch; the Qumran literature—it is all looking to the "breakthrough" of an apocalyptic figure who himself would never know suffering.

We find, it is true, "the tribulation of the Messiah," but this was not something that would touch the Messiah himself but rather something which the community would endure, and from which and after which, the Messiah would appear. At Qumran there is found a beautiful text in the *holioth* in which the *community* is represented like a woman in travail. She is going through the messianic tribulations; she is suffering, and only afterwards will the Messiah appear.

When the Apostles, therefore, insisted with firm conviction that Jesus was really and truly the *Kyrios,* a problem arose. Why had He ever suffered? Why had their own priests condemned Him? That was something for which the Apostles had to apologize. They do not perceive any instrinsic efficacy in the Passion as we do today. For them the Passion was something mysterious; they explained it in only two ways:

First, God had foreordained it. It was His will. And when God wills something, man does not ask questions. Through the early instructions of Jesus and the illumination of Pentecost, the Apostles recognized the direction of Old Testament prophecies about the servant of the Lord. In the book of Isaia, God had foretold the sufferings of the Messiah.

There was, on the other hand, a second element in their apologetic: Jesus was in no wise responsible for His death. It was the malevolence of men that had caused it.

And so it was, therefore, that the earliest consecutive story in primitive Christianity was the Passion story. The earliest concatenation of events centered in the Passion. Why? Because the Apostles needed an apologetic.

They had to show that in every step of the Passion, our Lord was victimized by enemies. A traitorous disciple betrayed Him. Jealous priests schemed against him. The Jewish tribunal, the Sanhedrin, was unable to find fault with Him. In the trial before Pilate, the Jews twisted the accusation and so caused His death.

The same is true of Stephen's sermon in the seventh chapter of Acts. He simply rehearses the history of Israel. Moses was rejected by his brethren. Joseph was subject to the jealousy of his brothers. The prophets all suffered from their compatriots. Why, then, were the Jews scandalized that this man Jesus was rejected by His brethren? Why were they incredulous if this crucified Jesus was glorified by God as the risen Savior?

In order to show the malevolence of men the text in Psalm 117 was frequently cited in the apostolic Church: "The stone which the builders rejected has itself become the cornerstone" (Acts 4:11; Rom. 9:33; Mk. 12:10). It was thus shown that violent rejection by His own was actually foretold in the Scriptures.

These, then, were the elements of the apologetic which the Apostles brought forward: everything under the control of God's will; everything predicted in the "suffering servant" prophecies; everything already foretold about his rejection by His own.

We owe it to St. Paul that a new dimension was brought into the Church's thinking on the passion of Christ. St. Paul did not come to this new aspect of the Passion through meditation or contemplation but through the contingencies of his apostolate.

In the beginning, Paul, like everyone else, held to the kerygma; he preached the Resurrection and the Parousia. Those were his cardinal doctrines everywhere. They clearly show up in his sermon at Pisidian Antioch (Acts 13:16ff.). During his second missionary journey his preaching faithfully followed the lines of the apostolic kerygma. After revisiting the Churches of Asia Minor, he crossed into Macedon. There he began to evangelize the whole Grecian territory. At Philippi he was momentarily successful, but before long he met opposition from the Judeo-Christians. They hounded him from the city, forcing him to flee to Thessalonica.

At Thessalonica, he achieved initial success in sowing the seed of faith, but persecution soon shattered the peace. This time he fled to Berea. Here he preached and established a very fervent community, much in love with the Scriptures. But the Judeo-Christians appeared once more, and he had to flee to the south. He next showed up at Athens.

At Athens he went into the Aeropagus, and again preached the Resurrection and the Parousia. He quoted the Greek poets; he reasoned with their logic; he used all their oratorical devices. When he rose to the culmination of his preaching, when he announced that Jesus was risen from the dead they stifled yawns and told him that they would listen to him some other time. At Athens he could count as converts only Damaris, Dionysius and a few others (Acts 17:32ff.).

He was now on his way over to Corinth. At this moment Paul was a broken man. At Athens he had used all his oratorical power and failed miserably. What then was to happen at Corinth? He was facing a wide-open seaport town, a people riddled with lust. If he had failed with the learned Athenians, how could he ever succeed among these depraved Corinthians?

At the same time he was very much worried about the fate of the Churches which he had left behind. In fact, he tells us in his letter to the Thessalonians that he had sent Timothy back to these Churches while he himself went on down to Corinth. He was afraid "lest perhaps, the tempter should tempt you and our labor come to naught" (1 Thess. 3:5).

Timothy finally returned to him and reported that at Thessalonica everything was going beautifully! At that moment Paul began looking back over his apostolate and seeing it in an entirely new light. Wherever he had gone to plant the seed, there had been suffering and persecution, and yet the seed had grown. In weakness there had been power; in suffering there had actually been a cleaving to the Word of God. It gave him a new insight into God's way of acting. He began then, perhaps for the first time, to realize the tremendous fact that God's favorite area to work in is human weakness.

This is all brought out in Paul's first Epistle to the Thessalonians. "We know, brethren, beloved of God, how you were chosen." He has just received the message of Timothy.

They are suffering, they are boycotted, but it makes no difference, for they are cleaving to the faith. "Our gospel was not delivered to you in word only, but in power also, and in the Holy Spirit, and in much fullness, as indeed you know what manner of men we have been among you for your sakes. And you became imitators of us and of the Lord, receiving the word in great tribulation" (1 Thess. 1:4-7).

He recognizes how active has been the Word of God in those who believed. "For you, brethren, have become imitators of the churches of God which are in Judea in Christ Jesus, in that you also have suffered the same things from your own countrymen as they have" (1 Thess. 2:14).

Looking back over every Church which he had founded, he saw human weakness and divine power—suffering and glory! Steeped in the writings of Isaia as Paul was, he could benefit from what he saw. St. Paul, in fact, has often been called "The Isaia of the New Testament." If there is one truth which is cardinal in Isaia, it is this: Only when a man is intensely conscious of his weakness can he be filled with the power of God. Only when man has given up clinging to human things as being sources of salvation and emptied himself of proud self-reliance, can the power of God rush in.

The whole order of God's Salvation as Isaia had revealed it was this: When Israel had become a charred stump, a bare handful, leveled to the earth, then only would the new seed of the Messiah rise to glorify the nation. "The destruction he has decreed, the Lord, the God of hosts, will carry out within the whole land. . . . But a shoot shall sprout from the stump of Jesse, and from his roots a bud shall blossom. . . . The Lord shall again . . . reclaim the remnant of his people" (Is. 10:23; 11:1, 11).

Now Paul could see this same principle at work in Christ. In Christ, too, was this combination of weakness and of strength, this union of suffering and of glory. From now on, Paul will preach that through the Cross one comes to the light.

Coming to Corinth, therefore, after his frustrating experience at Athens, Paul says to them: "I determined not to know anything among you, except Jesus Christ and him crucified" (1 Cor. 2:2). He has changed his message! It is no longer *Resurrection-Parousia,* but Passion-Resurrection. He will bring this out very beautifully in concluding his second letter to the Corinthians: Jesus "was crucified through weakness, yet he lives through the power of God" (2 Cor. 13:4).

This, however, is not the total explanation of Paul's thought. To stop there would utterly belie what is deepest and best and what is really the life-giving principle of his words. We would be in danger of slipping into this mentality: "So long as we fail, we shall succeed; so long as we are frustrated, then we shall be glorious; so long as we are incompetent workers, then God will do his best work; so long as we do nothing and become quietists, then God is left free."

If there is *any* thought contrary to Paul, it is this. This attitude would sanction laziness, encourage incompetence, and canonize Quietism. What, then, we ask, is Paul's full thought? If weakness begets God's strength, it is not because it is weakness; it is rather because in weakness the man of faith cleaves to God. In weakness this holding on to God is strongest so that man's soul is wide open to receive from God everything that God wants to give.

The Suffering Servant who cries out, "My God, my God, why have you forsaken me?" who is reduced, as it were, to an utter emptiness, is the very same one who says: "But, you, O Lord, be not far from me . . . hasten to help me" (Ps. 21:2, 20). Here we glimpse a cleaving unto the Lord; here is weakness opening its heart in love. This dependence upon God constitutes the intrinsic efficacy of weakness. But if love is missing, then the weakness is the weakness of sin, failure, and frustration, something that is utterly dead.

Paul sums up his thought in Philippians, where he beautifully says that even though Christ "was by nature God, [he] did not consider being equal to God a thing to be clung to, but emptied himself, taking the nature of a servant and . . . becoming obedient to death" (Phil. 2:6-8). God, therefore, exalted him through the Resurrection, giving him this name of Yahweh. At that name every knee should bend.

We must fully appreciate that word "therefore," because it contains all of Paul's thought. Because Christ emptied Himself, *therefore* God exalted Him. "Therefore" is more than a stylistic device; it means more than mere sequence of time, as though to say that there was weakness and then there was strength; first humiliation, then glory. This is not Paul's thought.

It is not even Paul's thought to say that "therefore" points to a reward: *because* He did this, the *reward* was given. No. The bond between the Passion and the Resurrection is much more intimate. The bond between the death and the glory is one of intrinsic causality. "I planted the seed, therefore the flower grew. . . . I planted the acorn, therefore from the intrinsic efficacy of that acorn the oak has come." As Father Stanislaus Lyonnet, S.J., a scholar with profound insight into St. Paul, expressed it: "The resurrection of Jesus is more a flowering forth from His death than merely the reward which the Eternal Father gave Him."

Today we know that the Resurrection and Passion together constitute one single objective act of Redemption. They are inseparably connected, like the concave and the convex of one and the same image. The Resurrection has come "causally" from the Passion, from its intrinsic necessity. And why?

For St. Paul the whole intrinsic necessity is found in agape—love. For him our Blessed Lord is One sent by the Father with a mission of love. He came to save us as a spiritual Messiah and to make us what we should be by this tremendous gift of His love. There was never any alteration in this love; it never grew, it never decreased. This love was the same from the beginning to the end: "Jesus is the same, yesterday, and today, yes, and forever" (Heb. 13:8).

This love of Jesus, our Savior, drove Him on to give His very best to his public life. Yet to represent Jesus as always looking forward to the Cross, like a man obsessed with the thought of death, is to be untrue to Him.

When our Lord came, He came with a work to do, and as a human being he gave His whole power to that work. He preached and labored among the people as though He were to accomplish His work in that way. It was love that was driving Him on. It was only when He saw exactly where this work was ending, that He realized humanly, that the fulfillment of the work would only be through His death. He, therefore, accepted the death. And He went forward to death with tremendous love, so that, as He put it so beautifully, "the world may know that I love the Father, and that I do as the Father has commanded me" (John 14:31).

Our Blessed Lord knew that what He could not accomplish by dynamic activity here upon earth, He could accomplish once He had passed through the *transitus* of death and had become the messianic Son of God.

An example might make it clear: A mother has a very wayward daughter. The mother loves the girl and she does everything she possibly can to gain her back. She rebukes her; she instructs her; she encourages her; she shows her all the love that she can. And yet, with all her best efforts, she fails. And then she realizes that if only she could be with God, that if only she could go through death and actually come before the throne of God, with all the power of someone who is now living as a saint with God, that then she could help her daughter as she never could in this life. And so it is, therefore, that she offers herself to die.

The mother is not seeking death; God is not pleased by death. Neither is it suffering which she is looking for; no one wants suffering, God least of all. What she longs for are life, power, and the full flowering forth of love. With God she can do for those whom she loves what she was never able to do before.

And so it was that this agape, the gift of the Holy Spirit in our Lord's human soul, drove Him on through life and through death, so that in very truth He was always looking forward to the moment when passing through death and giving up everything in the experience of death he could become our risen messianic Lord, could pour forth upon us the Spirit, and could do through that gift what He was never able to do so long as He was bound by the human limitations of His incarnation.

The soul of Christ united to the Divine Word passed through death bearing the identical love which had always been there during His lifetime. And at that moment of death He left behind Him the limitations of weak, human, mortal nature, so that His love was able, as it were, to erupt into a vast conflagration, no longer bound by the limitations of life upon earth, powerful as the glorified humanity of Him who is the very Son of God.

So often, therefore, when St. Paul writes of the death of Christ, two expressions keep recurring: "He loved me," and "He gave Himself for me."

He loved me, and therefore He went down to death in order that love, because it was love, could become dynamically active when He would rise from the dead as the glorious messianic Son of God.

In this He has proven His love for us, because when as yet we were sinners and unworthy of His love, He laid down His life for us (cf. Rom. 5:8). He died so that He could become the risen Savior and pour out upon the Church the fullness of the Spirit.

It is the light of this mystery of our Lord's death and resurrection, of His suffering and of His life, of the love which led Him to die and to suffer, and the love which leads Him to give everything to us today as the risen Savior—it is in this that we ourselves begin to understand the mystery of our own Christian life.

Our Baptism incorporates us into Christ in such a way that we become "other Christs." The Spirit who guided our Lord, the Spirit who illumined Him, the Spirit who charged His soul with love, is the same Spirit who reproduces that same love in our own life through the mystery of our Christian incorporation.

This is why for Paul the whole meaning of the Christian life is love. For Paul there is no law. All law has been abrogated—not merely the ceremonial, ritual law of Judaism, but *all law*. Now the Christian knows only one prin-

ciple of action, and that principle of action is totally from
within—the love, the agape, which the Spirit is infusing.
Ask a mother what law she is following in washing dishes
and in making beds, and she will look at you in amaze-
ment. She will say, "Why, I'm doing it because I love
them!" There is no law so exacting as love.

Thus it is, Paul tells us, that to all who are in Christ
Jesus there is no law. The only principle we know is this
tremendous agape which is within us, which is urging us
on to the very same kind of life that Christ lived. This
theme Paul develops at great length in the Epistle to the
Romans, chapter 3, and again in the Epistle to the Galatians, chapter 5. He tells us there, "if we live by the spirit,
then we must walk by the spirit" (Gal. 5:25). "The fruit
of the spirit," we are informed, "is charity, joy, peace,
patience, kindness, benignity." In other words, he draws
a perfect portrait not only of our own character as Christians, but a perfect portrait of the character of Jesus.

St. Paul tells us often, "Rejoice in the Lord always;
again I say, rejoice" (Phil. 4:4). He insists that peace and
joy are essential in the Christian life. All of this flows from
the fact that we have in us the very agape which Christ
had, given by the Spirit, and that this peace, this joy, is
something which we can always look forward to, because
the Spirit will know the full result of His activity.

At the same time, however, in this life this agape must
function in a world of weakness and of sin, not only around
us, but within us. As St. Paul expressed it, even though
we are living in the spirit, at the same time we are also
living in the flesh. We bear about with us a certain mortality, a pull of gravity, as it were, turning us in on ourselves, turning us away from God.

The liturgy speaks of the "pondus propriae actionis"—

the weight of our poor humanness that is always twisting us, as it were, to selfishness and away from God. Now, our Lord knew that same "pondus," that same pull of humanness. He was "tempted" to give people what they wanted, to meet their need for excitement and pleasure. This easy way of meeting needs was opposed by the hard way which the Father required. And Jesus kept clinging to the Father, which meant a constant cross in His life: the vertical pull to the will of the Father, the horizontal pull to the desires of His people.

We are in a similar situation. We know the will of God, the vertical pull in life, and at the same time we feel the horizontal pull of our mortality, our "flesh," the needs of our human nature. The agape is always trying to lift us up in fidelity, but it is always being dragged down by the pull of our poor humanness. In such lives the Cross is inevitable. The agape is not only responsible for introducing the Cross, it also gives it meaning.

This is the secret of our Lord's life, as Paul saw it; and it is the secret of the Christian life as we must live it. Mortification and self-denial, all those negative factors of life are without meaning if they are not prompted by agape. Our Lord could become all things to all men, He could forget Himself completely because there was this driving urge to love. And those who have followed Him have been given this same spirit.

When Paul was at Rome in prison, word was brought to him that some of his colleagues were taking advantage of his imprisonment to preach among the people and gain a following for themselves that would rival Paul's. Those who reported this back to Paul expected him to be depressed at the prospect of losing his hold on his favorite converts. Paul's reaction to these reports showed no depression, no effort to "mortify his pride"; it was simply: "What of it? So long as Christ is being preached! In this I rejoice, yes, and I will rejoice!"

When there is this driving agape, the negative elements in life are reduced to secondary importance. Many examples can be drawn from everyday life. If we must walk a long distance in bitterly cold weather, we can say that we are mortifying ourselves. But this "mortification," by itself, will give us neither joy nor peace, but only chilblains, pain, and depression.

On the other hand, if agape prompts us to remember a sick person to be helped, then, of course, there is joy and there is peace. This line of thinking does something to the whole spiritual life. We no longer have our little set forms of mortification which we hold to like fetishes. Agape becomes the ruling principle in life. That was the way Paul saw our Lord's life; that is the way he helps us to see ours.

Paul sums it all up, writing to the Philippians of our fellowship in the sufferings of Christ: "The things that were gain to me, these, for the sake of Christ, I have counted loss. Nay more, I count everything loss because of the excelling knowledge of Jesus Christ, my Lord. For his sake I have suffered the loss of all things, and I count them as dung that I may gain Christ and be found in him, not having a justice of my own, which is from the Law, but that which is from faith in Christ, the justice from God based upon faith; so that I may know him and the power of his resurrection and the fellowship of his sufferings" (Phil. 3:7-10).

In speaking of the fellowship of the sufferings of Christ, Paul did not mean to say: "I, standing here, look upon Jesus there, and imitate Him." No, he meant something infinitely deeper. He meant that the fellowship of the sufferings of Christ comes from this truth: that the very Spirit which was in Jesus, charging His soul with agape and driving Him on to endure everything because He loved us, is in us, charging us with agape to go and do everything we possibly can to show our love for God and our love for men.

Our union with Him and our imitation of Him is not merely a psychological adjustment of our minds to what He did. Nor must we duplicate exactly the kind of suffering which Jesus endured. The fundamental thing is that we are interiorly united, so that I am really and truly Jesus, because His Spirit is really and truly my Spirit.

CHAPTER 6 # THE FELLOWSHIP OF HIS SUFFERINGS

Through conversion St. Paul gained a new spiritual life. On the road to Damascus he received from the risen Christ the messianic gift of the Holy Spirit who ever after inspired and ruled his activity as that of a true son of God. For the Apostle this meant, in the expressive phrase of Philippians 3:10, that he had come to know Christ, "in the power of his resurrection." But that was not all. He affirms in the same breath that, through conversion, he came to know also "the fellowship of his sufferings." This significant addition is in accord with the polarity of all Pauline thought which joins death and resurrection as two inseparable aspects of the same salvific mystery, whether in the life of Christ or in the lives of Christians.

It is not easy, however, to determine the precise application of this death theme to the enigmatic phrase, "the fellowship of his sufferings," for the context does not define or explain its authentic meaning. Paul, moreover, has spoken so rarely of the historical details of the Passion that the expression, "sufferings of Christ," fails to command the unanimous interpretation accorded to words of obvious meaning.

Due to this uncertainty, the controverted phrase needs to be studied in the light of Paul's general doctrine, especially as it is found in the great epistles of Corinthians, Galatians and Romans. For when he wrote Philippians, Paul had already advanced beyond the limitations of the early kerygma — the apostolic preaching in the first year after Pentecost — and even beyond the limitations of his own doctrine in his first epistles, those to the Thessalonians. During the first months at Corinth, he went through a maturing process which virtually developed his thought and significantly influenced his preaching. This enrichment is reflected in the epistles which followed. Their fullness constitutes the background of his words in Philippians. Hence a review and examination of relevant themes in the Pauline corpus will help greatly to explain his affirmation that conversion brought him to know Christ and "the fellowship of his sufferings."

The doctrine on suffering in First and Second Thessalonians reflects the teaching of the primitive church as enunciated in Acts 14:21: "Through many tribulations must we enter the kingdom of God." In accord with this truth, Paul takes it for granted that the Christian lives in a climate of suffering. He insinuates this in an opening phrase of his first letter to the Thessalonians and frequently alludes in both letters to the sufferings borne by himself and his Thessalonian converts. Thus he employs many forms of *thlipsis,* a Greek word more and more frequently used for those tribulations which usher in the glorious Risen Christ.

Such suffering is not a mere accident; rather, it is a necessity imposed by divine decree, for in First Thessalonians Paul parallels his earlier statement in Acts with the equivalent phrase, "we are *bound* to suffer." Even though the struggle between good and evil will break out in titanic fury at the end of time, still it has already begun: the "Tempter" is active; the "mystery of iniquity" is at work (*cf.*, 2 Thess. 2:1 ff.). Hence, for Paul, there is no break in continuity between the sufferings of the present moment and the eschatological crisis of the final age of the world.

This explains the rich joy which the Thessalonians and Paul himself experienced in their trials. Looking forward eagerly to the imminent coming of Christ, they were able to identify their trials as a share in the tribulations of the "last age." Hence, their hope was something more than ordinary hope; it was an attitude of patient and persevering waiting in the midst of trials. In the New Testament this virtue is always, at least implicitly, connected with messianic salvation, for it represents the power of hope to endure in the midst of sufferings which lead to final reward. The patient endurance of trials, therefore, fills the Christian with joy, for it brings the conviction that such fidelity in the midst of messianic tribulations provides a pledge of salvation at the time of the *Parousia* or the second coming of the Risen Lord.

This doctrine of the Epistles to the Thessalonians might lead one to conclude that Paul's teaching on suffering is identical with that of contemporary Judaism: i.e., the patient endurance of trial is really a blessing, for it is only by passing righteously through the messianic throes that one will enter the messianic kingdom. Fragmentary references in these letters show, however, that Paul thinks of suffering in a *Christian* light: trials are the continuation of the tribulations which Christ himself inaugurated. What is more, these references, when coupled with other doctrinal elements in these epistles, suggest a concept which Paul will develop later. The bond between the sufferings of the Chritian and Christ is based on intimate union.

In Thessalonians Paul speaks of the suffering Christians as "imitators" of the suffering Christ. As St. John Chrysostom points out, the term of comparison in 1 Thessalonians 1:6 is suffering with joy: "You became imitators of us and of the Lord, receiving the word in great tribulation, with joy of the Holy Spirit." A second text which is more casual in its reference to Christ, centers the comparison in suffering alone: "For you, brethren, have become imitators of the churches of God which are in Judea in Christ Jesus, in that you also have suffered the same things from your own countrymen as they have . . ." (1 Thess. 2:14). To explain this bond it would suffice to invoke the dominant theme of these letters with regard to suffering and to conclude that the conformity between the suffering Christ and the suffering Christian arises from their common adherence to the design of God that all who attain messianic glory must pass through messianic trial. There are indications, however, that Paul's concept of imitating Christ involves a more intimate bond.

It is significant that the word "imitator" always denotes moral effort in the New Testament. It reflects the saying of Jesus: "If anyone wishes to come after me, let him deny himself, and take up his cross, and follow me" (Mk. 8:34). We see a close connection with the concept of a disciple following his master. This theme of master-disciple is actually found in First Thessalonians, where Paul makes clear that the precepts governing Christian life have come from God through and in Christ Jesus (4:2f.: 5:18). He is, therefore, the mediator of God's will and the master of all who are subject to it. It is noteworthy that, to express this role of Christ, Paul uses the phrase "in Christ Jesus" which recurs through these two letters and which, at least in the following epistles, frequently refers to an intrinisic bond.

Even in the present epistles, moreover, Paul shows Christ forming his disciples by actual influence from within. He writes in First Thessalonians: "May the Lord make you to increase and abound in charity . . . that he may strengthen your hearts, blameless in holiness before God our Father, at the coming of our Lord Jesus Christ" (1 Thess. 3:12f.). In his first epistles, therefore, Paul's concept of imitating Christ in suffering may be based not only on the duty of the Christian to follow the same divine will that imposed messianic suffering on the Savior, but also on the intrinsic necessity of living the pattern of life that flows inevitably from inward communion with Him who, while on earth, suffered the trials of the Messiah.

There is also another suggestive element in these early letters. Paul asserts that the joy of suffering with which the Christian imitates Christ is a gift of the Holy Spirit. "You have become imitators of us and of the Lord . . . with joy of the Holy Spirit" (1 Thess. 1:6). This is significant, for the Holy Spirit is present in the Christian as God's permanent gift (*cf.*, 1 Thess. 4:8). The way is thus prepared for the subsequent Epistle to the Romans, wherein Paul teaches that the Christian has reason to rejoice in trial since he can rely on the ever-present Spirit to strengthen his resistance and to fulfill his hope (Rom. 5:3-5).

There is yet a last phrase to suggest that, even in Thessalonians, Paul anticipated his later doctrine on the profound influence of Christ in all Christian suffering. He writes: "May the Lord direct your hearts into the love of God and the patience of Christ" (2 Thess. 3:5). As it stands, the phrase is open to several interpretations.

J. E. Frame (*Epistles of St. Paul to the Thessalonians,*

p. 296) suggests that it refers to Christ not only as the supreme model but also as the efficient cause of the Christian's patience. Paul, therefore, asks here that his converts may be strengthened with a patience that is both inspired by the example of Christ and actually bestowed by Him.

B. Rigaux (*Les Epîtres aux Thes.*, 700) and M. Zerwick (*Graecitas Biblica*, 12), while accepting this explanation of Frame, enrich it by interpreting the phrase in the light of Paul's doctrine on the union of Christ with His members. Seen in this light, the patience which Paul requests for his converts is truly "Christ's patience," not only because He bestows it but also because He, as the "Body," must claim whatever belongs to His members. There is much to recommend this thoroughly Pauline interpretation. Not only is it warranted by Paul's allusions in Thessalonians to the bond between Christ and His followers, it is also a corollary of the words spoken to Paul in his inaugural vision: "Saul, Saul, why dost thou persecute me? . . . I am Jesus whom thou art persecuting" (Acts 9:4-5).

Such allusions to a distinctly Pauline explanation of suffering, though precious, are only fragmentary and incidental; as such, they leave much room for discussion. The fact is that in these first two epistles Paul does not emphasize the role of Christ in *present* life and suffering. His attention is fastened on the Parousia or final coming, and his thought is strongly colored by the eschatological outlook of late Judaism and early Christianity. Hence it may be that in Thessalonians he is content to emphasize only that aspect of the bond between Christ and the Christian which is based on God's will ordaining trial both for the messiah and his followers as the necessary means for entering the kingdom.

Passing now to the period of the great Epistles of First

and Second Corinthians, Galatians, and Romans, we notice a marked shift of emphasis from the outlook and teaching of Thessalonians. Paul's own experience offers the probable reason for this new development. Leaving Thessalonica, he went to Athens where, in his address at the Areopagus, he followed the pattern of his earlier preaching (Acts 17:16-31). Not only did he develop the theme of resurrection-parousia, but he also embellished his words with oratorical devices. This method of preaching met with signal failure so that, coming to Corinth immediately afterwards, he feared even worse (1 Cor. 2:1-3). But now he deliberately altered the theme of his discourse to emphasize the role of the death of Christ in God's plan for salvation. He also changed to a simple style of preaching and addressed especially the less promising elements of the population.

As the months passed, Paul witnessed a phenomenon which made a deep impression upon him. He had already seen at Thessalonica that spiritual fruitfulness was possible even under a storm of suffering. Now at Corinth he came to see that suffering and human weakness provide the climate that is most conducive to the activity of God's saving power. He was not slow to grasp the implications of this experience. It squared perfectly with the Isaian picture of Redemption. Salvation did not depend upon human strength but only upon God, so that all glory belongs to him alone:

> The haughty eyes of man will be lowered,
>   the arrogance of men will be abased,
>   and the Lord alone will be exalted on that day.
> By waiting and by calm you shall be saved,
>   in quiet and in trust your strength lies.
>   (Is. 2:11; 30:15)

This principle of "salvation through God alone" pervades biblical thought, appears frequently in non-biblical Jewish literature, and finds some of its most beautiful expressions in the hymns of Qumran. In one of these hymns, as translated by Menahem Mansoor, we read:

> For I know that truth are the words of thy mouth and in Thy hand is righteousness, and in Thy thought is
> All knowledge; and in Thy power is all might and all glory is with Thee. In Thy wrath are all judgments of affliction,
> But in Thy goodness there is abundance of forgiveness, and Thy mercies are on all Thy favored sons. For Thou hast made known to them Thy true counsel,
> And through Thy marvelous mysteries Thou hast enlightened them. And for the sake of Thy glory, Thou hast cleansed man from transgression so that he may consecrate himself
> For Thee . . .
>
> (IQH 11:7-11)

Paul himself recognized this principle at work in the unfolding of the divine plan at Corinth. Human weakness and human contradiction provided the ambient for fruitful divine activity, that all might recognize and give glory to the true author of salvation. At Corinth the Apostle came to see in a new way that men must become aware of their own human powerlessness if they are to make room for the power of God. Trial and weakness, therefore, because they lead to such awareness, are both a preparation for and a sign of God's work.

Paul returns to this theme time and again in the first three chapters of First Corinthians. He identifies it as the governing principle in the divine choice of the crucifixion of Christ for the work of salvation; God has chosen what is humanly "weak" and "foolish" to accomplish His greatest mercy, that men might see clearly how fully the power and wisdom of salvific activity is all His. In this new emphasis on the death of Christ as interpretative of the nature of the salvific plan, Paul delivered the very "testimony of God" (1 Cor. 2:1). He focussed attention on the human "weakness" of the way in which Christ attained messianic glory and so demonstrated that salvation is wholly God's work and wholly a work of love.

The Apostle saw this principle of power-in-weakness directing also the extension of salvific activity through his own preaching: "It pleased God, by the foolishness of our preaching, to save those who believe" (1 Cor. 1:21). The same principle was at work in the selection of the first converts: "The foolish things of the world has God chosen to put to shame the 'wise,' and the weak things . . . and the despised . . . and the things that are not" (1 Cor. 1:27-29). Moreover, to counter the arrogance of the Corinthians who were preening themselves as though they had attained the fullness of salvation, Paul emphasized the fact that the apostles in whom God's power is most active experience an acute feeling of human insufficiency and suffer great trials constantly.

Nowhere, perhaps, does Paul express this reaction so poignantly than in Second Corinthians: "We carry this treasure in vessels of clay, to show that the abundance of the power is God's and not ours. In all things we suffer tribulation, but we are not distressed; we are sore pressed, but we are not destitute; we endure persecution, but we are not forsaken; we are cast down, but we do not perish; always bearing about in our body the dying of Jesus, so that the life also of Jesus may be made manifest in our body. For we the living are constantly being handed over to death for Jesus' sake, that the life also of Jesus may be made manifest in our mortal flesh" (2 Cor. 4:7-11).

Thus, always and everywhere, God manifests His power in a context of human weakness. The reason remains ever the same: Men must learn that all spiritual strength comes from God alone and can be used only with His help, "so that, just as it is written, 'let him who takes pride, take pride in the Lord' " (1 Cor. 1:31).

The shift of emphasis in First Corinthians from resurrection-parousia to death-resurrection is accompanied by new attention to the riches and requirements of Christian life *here on earth*. Succeeding epistles will concentrate more and more on this, until, in the later captivity epistles, Paul's attention rests almost entirely on the anticipated resurrection which union with Christ brings even in this life. But these subsequent developments are already contained substantially in the teaching of First Corinthians. There he writes of the Christian's present union with Christ and of the dynamic activity of the Spirit whom he bestows. "Flee immorality," he demands. "Every sin that a man commits is outside the body, but the immoral man sins against his own body. Or do you not know that your body is the temple of the Holy Spirit, who is in you, whom you have from God, and that you are not your own? For you have been bought at a great price. Glorify God in your body" (1 Cor. 6:18-20).

This doctrine of First Corinthians, however, is not complete; it must be complemented by the teaching of Romans and Galatians. For in these two letters Paul penetrates the involvements and applications of union with Christ which comes to the Christian through the Spirit at the moment of Baptism.

To appreciate the doctrine of these epistles one must

keep in mind that Paul is the "witness of the Resurrection" par excellence. In his account before King Agrippa of the miraculous event on the day of his conversion, he recalls Christ's words, "I have appeared to thee for this purpose, to appoint thee to be a minister and a witness to what thou hast seen, and to the visions that thou shalt have of me" (Acts 26:16). Paul remained true to this awareness of the Savior. Christ was always, for him, someone present and living. His constant allusion to Christian life as life "in Christ" serves as the classic emblem of his own conviction that Christians have been incorporated by Baptism into the body of the risen Christ.

Equally fundamental in his thought is the truth that Christ died and rose again, not merely as an individual but as the embodiment and representative of all men. The Hebrew conception of "corporate personality," essential for understanding Old Testament messianic prophecies, is essential also to Paul's concept of the role of Christ. Like Adam He, too, is a "corporate personality," a new Adam. Paul writes: "For as in Adam all die, so in Christ all will be made to live. . . . Even as we have borne the likeness of the earthly [man], let us bear also the likeness of the heavenly [man]" (1 Cor. 15:22, 49). Through the law of solidarity His death and resurrection are efficacious for all: "We have come to the conclusion that, since one died for all, therefore all died" (2 Cor. 5:14).

The efficacy of Christ's redemptive act takes effect in the individual through the rite of Baptism which is at once "a tomb and a womb." At Baptism, according to Paul's thought, the body-person of the Christian is united to the body-person of Christ. (This doctrine will be explained further in chapter nine.) Here we sense the physical realism of Old Testament thought which always considered the "body" not a part of man in contrast to the soul but the whole man as a concrete reality. The body, consequently, has an important role in the Old Testament prophecies of the final salvation. In Paul's thought, therefore, baptismal union takes place between two real, physical persons, the individual Christian and the individual glorified Christ.

These factors serve to explain the Apostle's words on the union of the baptized with the death of Christ: "Do you not know that all we who have been baptized into Christ Jesus have been baptized into his death?" (Rom. 6:3). In the simple realism of Paul's thought, Baptism so unites the body-person of the Christian to the body-person of the glorious Christ that He, who died and rose again as a corporate personality, is able to share with His members the salvific effects of His death and resurrection.

For Paul, as C. H. Dodd expresses it, "the whole sacrament is an act by which the believer enters into all that Christ did as his representative in that he was delivered up for our sins, and rose again for our justification" (*The Epistle to the Romans,* p. 87). Paul explained what it meant to share through Baptism in the effects of Calvary. The Christian is freed from subjection to the law, from the shackles of the "body of sin," from servile obedience to the world, from the death of sin. In a word, he is liberated with the "freedom wherewith Christ has made us free" (Gal. 4:31).

In order to understand Paul's conception of this truth and its application to Christian life, it is necessary to keep in mind an essential doctrine — that the death of Christ was a death of obedience and love. It brought an end to His bondage "in sinful flesh . . . under the law" (Rom. 8:3). His death, however, was not merely a negation of contact with the world; it was prompted and accompanied by an interior act of consummate obedience to the Father and of ardent love for men inspired by the Holy Spirit. His death was, above all else, a visible expression of the surrender of His whole humanity to the will of the Father who sent Him to die out of love for men (Rom. 5:6-8). The dynamism of such a death, vital with love and obedience, could never die. Once He had passed through death and escaped the limitations of life on earth, this abiding spirit found full and necessary expression in the messianic glorification of the Savior rising from the dead. Far from being a mere extrinsic reward, His glorious resurrection and salvific activity as messianic Son of God are the vital products and full flowering of the love and obedience which filled His soul in its passage through death.

This aspect of Christ's death-resurrection helps to explain a striking feature of St. Paul's doctrine on Baptism. For him sacramental death marks the point of departure for an altogether new life, in which the Christian ever remains "dead to sin, but alive to God" (Rom. 6:11). This is possible only because, in Baptism, the Christian shares the very Spirit of Christ which endures forever in the body-person to which the new member is united. If, therefore, baptismal incorporation brings death to the old life through the power of Christ's death, it is because the Spirit who prompted the loving obedience of His death now becomes active in the new member, transforming him radically from the carnal state of egoism to the spiritual state of God-mindedness. "It is now no longer I that live, but Christ lives in me. And the life that I now live in the flesh, I live in the faith of the Son of God, who loved me and gave himself up for me" (Gal. 2:20).

This concept of Baptism influences the whole Pauline program of Christian life. Because the baptized always remain members of the body of Christ, the power of His Spirit is ever present to keep them centered in God and dead to sin and to self. Life in Christ requires this: "Thus do you consider yourselves as dead to sin, but alive to God in Christ Jesus" (Rom. 6:11).

It is in chapter eight of Romans that Paul penetrates deeply into the workings of this death principle. He makes clear that the Holy Spirit, received in Baptism, is always active in the Christian, guiding him with vital inspirations that deliver him from the tyranny of sin and death; for "the inclination of the Spirit is life and peace." Because he is the "Spirit of Christ," His every gift conforms the baptized to the image of the Son. This means that "they who are led by the Spirit are sons of God"; for the Spirit infuses into them the Son's love for the Father. This love always inclines to the Father's will; and so, by its very nature, it is a principle of opposition to the "flesh." "The wisdom of the flesh is hostile to God, for it is not subject to the law of God, nor can it be." "Flesh," in Paul's language, includes everything in man hostile to God.

Flesh turns man away from God, and leads to sin and death. But by conserving and strengthening in the baptized the Son's love for His Father, the Spirit leads man to wage ceaseless war on the deeds of the flesh. In every conscious act the Christian must continue, through the power of the Spirit, to sacrifice all resistance which still remains in the flesh. Hence Paul writes, "Brethren, we are debtors, not to the flesh, that we should live according to the flesh, for if you live according to the flesh, you will die; but if by the Spirit you put to death the deeds of the flesh, you will live" (Rom. 8:12-13). It is this principle which gives originality to the moral and ascetical doctrine of St. Paul.

The Apostle treats the same theme in Galatians, where

he clearly attributes to the activity of the Holy Spirit the elimination of all that is evil in Christ's members: "Walk in the Spirit, and you will not fulfill the lusts of the flesh. . . . They who belong to Christ have crucified their flesh with its passions and desires. If we live by the Spirit, by the Spirit let us also walk" (Gal. 5:16, 24 f.). The word "crucified" is not a mere figure. Baptism gives a share in the death which loving fidelity to God's will produced in Christ, so that Paul could write, "With Christ I have been nailed to the cross" (Gal. 2:19). The continuance of the baptismal contact with the risen Savior fills the member of His body with the strong love that crucifies whatever is hostile to the will of God. "They who belong to Christ have crucified their flesh with its passions and desires" (Gal. 5:24).

Christian life, therefore, involves an enduring paradox. The Christian, on the one hand, lives on an eschatological plane, sharing the risen life of the Savior and His love for the Father. Paul writes in the name of every Christian, "I live, now not I, but Christ lives in me" (Gal. 2:20). On the other hand, the activity of the Holy Spirit has not yet transformed the whole of man, or the whole of the world around him. Therefore, the "now" of life upon earth combines the present temporal level with the final eschatological moment. As long as the Christian is in the world he must carry a "body of death"; he is always able to "yield his members to sin as weapons of iniquity"; he is constantly surrounded by "the wisdom of the flesh that is hostile to God." Hence, though he has truly "put on Christ" through Baptism, a weakness is always present to solicit a return to the earthly ways of his old self.

Paul was vitally aware that in the present life the Christian shares only imperfectly in his redemption. The Apostle, therefore, recognizes a constant tension between the two orders, eschatological and temporal. This awareness is reflected in his epistles; his language ceaselessly varies in them from the indicative mood of simple declaration, when he enunciates the truth that the Christian lives Christ's own life, to the imperative mood of command, when he urges his converts to fulfill the exigencies of the heavenly life. On the one hand, for example, he states the fact, "Our old self has been crucified with him"; yet immediately he goes on to command, "Therefore, do not let sin reign in your mortal body" (Rom. 6:6, 12).

The actual process of dying is always a painful experience, for it involves separation from what nature clings to. The death of Christ Himself was painful beyond measure; He had come "in the likeness of sinful flesh" and underwent real suffering when He had to part with it, in passing through the door of death to heavenly life. Once His passion was over and He had risen from the tomb, this "death was swallowed up in victory" (1 Cor. 15:54); for the love and obedience that filled His soul in the moment of death gained power to effect every good. In the application of this efficacy to His members upon earth, however, Christ must often renew the painful experience of mortal suffering. It is characteristic of His Spirit to separate His members from whatever does not accord with God's will — even though it be something as intimate as one's own "flesh" and as homelike as the "world." The daily "dying" of the Christian, therefore, is a prolongation of Christ's own death, just as the abnegation characteristic of Christian service is truly a sacrifice. Such experiences renew in the member that state of death which love and obedience produced in Christ. It is His Spirit, received in Baptism, who inspires and rules all.

In Romans and Galatians Paul affirms an intimate bond between the death of Christ and the inevitable conflict and suffering in each Christian's life. This bond rests on the truth, often repeated in these epistles, that the principle of death in both cases is one and the same. Because they are intimately united by Baptism as body and member, both Christ and the Christian share the same Holy Spirit whose activity inspires the death which loving obedience to God enjoins.

A study of the doctrine on suffering in Romans and Galatians must take into account Paul's statement in chapter eight of Romans. In these verses he brings together the theme of Romans on union with Christ in suffering and an earlier theme of Thessalonians, union with Him in the eschatological tribulation.

This text concludes Paul's analysis of the death principle which the baptized receives from Christ. Paul has identified it as the activity of the Holy Spirit, who infuses the life and love of the glorious Son of God, putting to death all that is inimical to God's will and insuring by His very presence the certainty of glorious resurrection. Paul then describes this *terminus* of Christian experience: "If we are sons, we are heirs also; heirs indeed of God and joint heirs with Christ, since we suffer with him that we may also be glorified with him. For I reckon that the sufferings of the present time are not worthy to be compared with the glory to come to be revealed in us" (Rom. 8:17f.).

The thought here is clear enough. Christian sonship, Paul asserts, leads inevitably to full reward through the sufferings which are intimately connected with life in Christ. He has already introduced in chapter five the theme of tribulation, as it develops virtue and leads to glory through the activity of the Holy Spirit. Now in chapter eight he analyzes the contents of this earlier statement and shows that Christian suffering, which has its source in the Spirit's constant war on the flesh, is the necessary consequence of all union with Christ. Furthermore, Paul carefully identifies the "sufferings of the present time" with the tribulations which precede the final, eschatological coming of the Lord. This quasi-technical expression in the Pauline vocabulary—sufferings *of the present time*—refers to the period of tension and trial between the two appearances of Christ. As the Apostle has shown before and as he repeats here, the share which the Christian has in the messianic trials insures an even greater share in the messianic reward.

Because Paul describes the "sufferings of the present time" as a "suffering with Christ," the question arises, what is the nature and measure of the Christian's union with Christ while he passes through the tribulations which Christ's death inaugurated?

As it stands, the term "suffering with" could be interpreted as focusing attention on a bond between the sufferings of Christians and the *historical* passion of the Savior. Though the Apostle has spoken of such a bond in First Thessalonians, he has left this theme undeveloped in his following epistles. Indeed, the only feature of Christ's earthly life on which he centers attention is His death—and this because it constituted with the Resurrection the unique cause of salvation. Hence, in treating of this death he does not ordinarily delay over external aspects but views it constantly in its redemptive role. He sees it, on the one hand, as the necessary counterpart of the Resurrection. Christ's passage from this world made possible His full messianic activity of Savior. On the other, he traces the involvements of Christ's death in the lives of His members; they share its efficacy through the activity of the Holy Spirit. As J. Moffatt observes, "For the Apostle, what was vital was not the Lord as a heroic individual; it was Christ dying and rising as One who bore in his own person the destiny of God's chosen people, Christ living as the Lord and Spirit in whom they actually shared and reproduced his death and resurrection within their own experience" (*The First Epistle of St. Paul to the Corinthians*, p. 188).

This estimate of Paul's doctrine is particularly relevant in interpreting the phrase "suffering with," or, as the Greek expresses it, *sym-paschomen,* "co-suffering." All similar compounds, in fact, referring directly to union between the Christian and Christ, must be similarly interpreted: co-dying; co-buried; co-rejoicing. It is noteworthy that the Apostle limits these expressions to union with Christ in the salvific mysteries of His death and risen life; he never extends this phraseology to the incidents of the Savior's earthly life, so as to speak of co-praying with Christ, co-fasting, or co-conquering temptation. This significant restriction is consonant with the whole burden of Paul's doctrine in Romans and Galatians. In these epistles he teaches that Baptism, by uniting the Christian to the Savior, confers a share in His death-resurrection. This union constitutes the essential redemptive experience of Christ the "corporate personality." Life begins with Baptism, what happened before that moment matters little.

Thus the Christian is not only *in* Christ but also dies and lives *with* Him. It is this latter aspect which finds rich expression in Paul's writing. We have already seen that it is the Spirit, received in Baptism, who makes the Christian die to all that is apart from God; like Christ and in Christ, he lives unto God. Hence, because both body and member share the same principle of life and death, Paul not only claims for Christ all that His member is and has, but he also attributes to the member a true share in the salvific death-resurrection of the Savior.

This must be kept in mind in analyzing the phrase "we co-suffer *with* Him." To interpret the term, as some have done, as affirming primarily an identity or bond of *resemblance* between Christian suffering and the suffering of the Passion does not accord with Paul's many uses of this compound: *co*-dying; *co*-buried. Paul consistently applies these expressions to inner union with Christ's death-resurrection in their salvific efficacy. Moreover, references to the historical sufferings of Christ are so incidental and so apart from the consistent Pauline motif of death-resurrection that their presence does not suffice to alter the obvious Paulinism of Romans 8:17: "If we co-suffer, we will also be co-glorified."

The denial that the historical sufferings of Christ are the primary term of reference does not exclude this reference altogether. The fact is that Paul's thought includes by implication a bond of resemblance between Christian suffering and the Savior's passion. For Christian suffering flows from the presence in man of the Holy Spirit and so is always characterized by the fruits of his activity: charity, joy, peace, patience (Gal. 5:22). Paul, accordingly, has explicitly pointed out that Christians must manifest the dispositions of Christ in meeting the trials of life. He has also expressed the desire that "the patience of Christ" may characterize the sufferings of his converts (2 Thess. 3:5). He was certainly aware, therefore, of the bond of resemblance between Christians and the suffering Christ; and he has spoken of this in his letter to the Thessalonians: "You became imitators . . . of the Lord, receiving the word in great tribulation, with joy of the Holy Spirit" (1 Thess. 1:6).

This theme, however, does not come to the fore in the death-resurrection couplet of Romans 8:17-18. Here he merely repeats what he has developed earlier: Christians, because they are incorporated into the body of Christ, share not only His life but also His death (Rom. 6). It must be noted, nonetheless, that the juxtaposition of verses 17 and 18 adds a real contribution. Each verse sheds light upon the other. "If we are sons, we are heirs also; heirs indeed of God and joint heirs with Christ, since we suffer with him that we may also be glorified with him. For I reckon that the sufferings of the present time are not worthy to be compared with the glory to come to be revealed in us." The second verse with its rich background in First and Second Thessalonians, shows how real are the trials involved in suffering with Christ; the other verse stresses the intimate bond which unites the Christian to Christ. The Christian today undergoes the tribulations of the final messianic age, an age which opened the Savior's death. Through this juxtaposition of themes the divine plan of messianic reward through messianic suffering finds its due place in the Christology which dominates all of Paul's thought.

In the highly personal Second Epistle to the Corinthians Paul does not enunciate new themes; but, as a master in complete possession of the doctrine affirmed in the other great epistles, he shows the vital influence of these principles, especially in the apostolate. The attack of critics upon his apostolic authority and his mode of procedure as a minister of the Gospel forced him to reflect on the antimony of his public life. In every respect it manifested both divine force and human weakness. He treats this theme from every angle in the two apologetic sections: 1:12—7:17 and chapters 10—13. Apostolic labor, like Christian life itself, must follow the rule of thumb for all divine activity: power through weakness so that all glory may belong to God alone.

Throughout this epistle he constantly emphasizes that,

though the apostle is the bearer of God's power, he carries this treasure in a vessel of clay. Apostolic life involves struggle and suffering; it leads to inward tension and outward persecution. Paul's own endeavor to bring the light of God to man involved a corresponding experience of human weakness. This aspect of his apostolate had been foretold of him from the beginning; the Lord said to Ananias: "I will show him how much he must suffer for my name" (Acts 9:16). And suffer he did. "Whoever would write the story of Paul the apostle," as J. Schneider observes, "must write the story of his sufferings." His intimate self-revelation in Second Corinthians is a tale of suffering from within and from without. Yet so certain was Paul that this weakness was the human concomitant of divine power acting in him and through him, that the experience of human limitations was for him a cause of joy: "Of myself I will glory in nothing save in my infirmities" (2 Cor. 12:5).

He recounts a personal experience in which God Himself confirmed the conviction that divine power works through human frailty. Paul was suffering from a "thorn in the flesh" and prayed for deliverance. God answered: "My grace is sufficient for thee, for strength is made perfect in weakness." Paul draws the obvious conclusion in words which echo chapter one of First Corinthians: "Gladly, therefore, I will glory in my infirmities that the strength of Christ may dwell in me. Wherefore I am satisfied, for Christ's sake, with infirmities, with insults, with hardships, with persecutions, with distresses. For when I am weak, then I am strong" (2 Cor. 12:9f.). In this epistle he also sums up in a brief statement the teaching that Christ himself had to follow the pattern which marks all divine activity —power through weakness: "For though he was crucified through weakness, yet he lives through the power of God" (2 Cor. 13:4).

But in Second Corinthians he does more than merely reiterate and apply the "power-weakness" theme of the first epistle. He here unites to it the vivid coloring of the principles enunciated in Romans and Galatians on the union of the Christian with Christ. Several passages are noteworthy.

The first of these passages is 2 Corinthians 1:3-7. "Blessed be the God and Father of Our Lord Jesus Christ, the Father of mercies and the God of all comfort, who comforts us in all our afflictions, that we also may be able to comfort those who are in any distress by the comfort wherewith we ourselves are comforted by God. For as the sufferings of Christ abound in us, so also through Christ does our comfort abound. For whether we are afflicted, it is for your instruction and salvation; or whether we are comforted, it is for your comfort; which shows its efficacy in the endurance of the selfsame sufferings that we also suffer. And our hope for you is steadfast, knowing that as you are partakers of the sufferings, so will you also be of the comfort."

Paul here repeats the familiar theme that afflictions abound in Christian life, and especially in the apostolic ministry. In accord, however, with the fundamental antithesis of death-resurrection, he affirms that such suffering brings its corresponding measure of comfort: "As the sufferings of Christ abound in us, so also through Christ does our comfort abound." Such comfort, it must be noted, is not merely personal; whatever the apostle experiences is of benefit to his converts. "Whether we are afflicted . . . or whether we are comforted," all serves to strengthen the Corinthians for the endurance of the same sufferings which the apostles sustain. Paul, therefore, is confident that because the Corinthians share his sufferings, they will share also the comfort which he has received.

The trials and sufferings of which he speaks are those that afflict both the apostle and his converts in the first days of a Christian community, for the Corinthians are true sharers in the tribulations which the founder of their Church endures. He describes his apostolic sufferings, in which the Corinthians share, as the "sufferings of Christ." It seems unlikely that the phrase identifies the sufferings of the Corinthians with the historical sufferings of the Passion. It is also unlikely that the phrase refers only to an *extrinsic* bond, based on Christ's command or the exigencies of His service. Rather, the dominance in Paul's doctrine of the *intrinsic* bond between the Christian and Christ strongly suggests that this expression contains richer meaning.

The Corinthians truly belong to Christ who, through His Spirit, is the efficient principle of all Christian experience in the lives of His members. This aspect, which is the immediate consequence of baptismal union with Christ, is the quality which gives richest value to the sufferings of both apostle and converts. Indeed, it is because the *fellowship of their sufferings* is really a *fellowship of the sufferings of Jesus* that Paul applies the death-resurrection theme of all his thought to establish the certainty that consolation will follow upon trials.

It is legitimate to conclude, therefore, that 2 Corinthians 1:3-7 belongs to the thought-pattern already enunciated in Romans: "If we are sons, we are heirs also: heirs indeed of God and joint heirs with Christ, provided, however, we suffer with him that we may also be glorified with him." Both passages affirm an objective and necessary bond between suffering-consolation and suffering-glory. At the same time, these passages refer the trials of Christians directly to Christ, calling them "the sufferings of Christ" and "suffering with Christ." The parallelism of these texts emphasizes that Paul sees verified through the whole course of Christian life the union with Christ in His death-resurrection which was first realized through Baptism. Baptismal union between the body and its members necessarily involves a life process. The Holy Spirit leads the Christian to renew constantly the death of Christ in order to continue living with His life. It is with this context in mind, therefore, that Paul speaks of Christian trials as "the suffering of Christ."

Another striking example of the death-life theme is in chapter four of Second Corinthians. Paul has just spoken of the light which he received as an apostle to communicate to others. He goes on to affirm that the power of his ministry is wholly God's, for the elements of his own temporal life contribute little to its efficacy. "We carry this treasure in vessels of clay, to show that the abundance of the power is God's and not ours." His own experience made him vitally aware of this duality: "In all things we suffer tribulation, but we are not distressed; we are sore pressed, but we are not destitute; we endure persecution, but we are not forsaken; we are cast down, but we do not perish." His interpretation of the profound meaning of these vicissitudes is significant. He traces these antitheses to his union with Christ, whose death is the source of apostolic suffering and whose life is the source of apostolic strength. For he sums up all by portraying apostles as "always bearing about in our body the dying of Jesus, so that the life also of Jesus may be made manifest in our bodily frame. For we the living are constantly being handed over to death for Jesus' sake, that the life also of Jesus may be made manifest in our mortal flesh."

These words indicate that more than an external bond links the human weakness and suffering of the apostles to

Christ. The daily trials of apostolic life borne for Christ
are identified as a bearing about of "the dying of Jesus."
This latter expression refers to the state of death which is
the enduring effect of baptismal death with Christ. This
Paul has already indicated in chapter six of Romans where
he stated that those who have sacramentally died with
Christ must ever after consider themselves dead. Because
this state of death involves a constant dying to the deeds of
the flesh, it issues necessarily in the activity of self-denial
and mortification. But, whether considered in its primary
meaning as a passive state of death or in its derived sense
of active mortification, this "dying" of the Christian is truly
that of Christ, because His Spirit is the effective principle
who constantly renews the Savior's death in all the members
of His body.

In these verses Paul also states in parallel clauses that
the suffering of the apostolic life is inseparably connected
with the apostle's manifestation of the life of Christ: "in
order that the life also of Jesus may be manifest." Paul
speaks here of the actual effects of the labor and suffering
of his apostolate. For the manifestation of life takes place
in an earthly state and benefits the Corinthians in the present life. The force of the verb "to be made manifest" cannot
be overlooked. Though scarcely appearing outside the
New Testament, it shows there an almost technical meaning, referring to the first or second coming of Christ, with
the just sharing His glory. Its use in the present case
expresses the truth that the life which the apostle diffuses
is the life of the risen Christ, "the power of his resurrection."
At the same time it suggests that apostolic activity is an
anticipated share in the Resurrection.

In Paul's eyes the apostolate is but an extension to others
of the life of Christ who already lives in His apostle. Its

purpose is to form Christ in men, that He may live in them just as he lives in Paul. Apostolic labor, therefore, follows the same law that governs the personal development of every Christian: life accompanied by death. Paul expressed the pattern of apostolic life this way: "Death is at work in us, but life in you."

In the apostolate the "zone of fulfillment" for Christ's power is enlarged. This means an equally extensive zone of opposition. The apostle has to enter into conflict with a wider "world"; he must "crucify" sin and the hostile flesh in the life of every convert. All this involves struggle and suffering, which Paul can truly call the "dying of Jesus" since He who dwells in the apostle and acts upon him through His Holy Spirit provides the effective principle for such struggle. To make Christ live in his converts, therefore, the apostle himself has to endure the death that Christ underwent to share His life with the world. The principle of death is always one and the same; only the time and manner of its application differs.

A few verses later in chapter four of Second Corinthians, Paul presents another aspect—the psychological—of the union between Christ and His members. Though it is true that Paul does not here speak explicitly of suffering, he brings into sharp focus, nonetheless, the active, psychological influence of the principle which accounts for all Christian suffering.

In the other great epistles he has already shown why all Christians must endure trial and struggle; through the indwelling of Christ's Spirit they share ontologically in the dynamic love-principle of Christ's activity. He now affirms that the very love which the Savior manifested in His life and ministry and which He now continues in His glorious life provides, also, the dynamic psychological impulse of the Christian apostolate: "The love of Christ impels us, because we have come to the conclusion . . . that Christ died for all, in order that they who are alive may live no longer for themselves, but for him who died for them and rose again" (2 Cor. 5:14f.).

Such fullness of ontological and psychological sharing in the inward spirit of the Savior is required by the very nature of the apostolate, for both Christ and His apostle are engaged in the same work of reconciliation under the guiding inspiration of God's love: "All things are from God, who has reconciled us to himself through Christ and has given to us the ministry of reconcilation. For God was truly in Christ, reconciling the world to himself. . . . On behalf of Christ, therefore, we are acting as ambassadors, God, as it were, appealing through us." This charge and its motivation in love flow from the inward bond between Christ and His members, the bond to which Paul has attributed the whole of Christian suffering.

The same thought of union with Christ in His death-resurrection underlies one of the concluding passages of Second Corinthians. "Do you seek a proof," Paul asks, "of the Christ who speaks in me, who is not weak in your regard, nay, is powerful in you? For he was crucified through weakness, yet he lives through the power of God. Yes, we also are weak in him, yet we shall live with him through the power of God in your regard" (13:3f.).

Paul here stabilizes the "power-weakness" theme of First Corinthians as the law of Christian life; he also identifies it with the intrinsic bond which unites Christians to Christ and gives them a share in his death-life.

Paul deals with the antinomy of His ministry: though personally weak, he is conscious of bearing the power of Christ. Such an experience is inevitable. For the Savior

Himself had to follow the law that governs all divine activity in this world: "He was crucified through weakness, yet he lives through the power of God." Therefore Paul, too, must follow this rule, not merely because it is a law of God's salvific activity, but especially because he lives by the very principle that produces death-life in both the body and its members. Whatever weakness or power the apostle experiences in doing God's work, all is both "in Christ" and "with Christ": "We also are weak *in Him,* yet we shall live *with Him* through the power of God in your regard."

This passage is a particularly felicitous conclusion to Second Corinthians, since it blends so well the themes of the two preceding epistles. It offers a consummate apologia for the "weakness" of the apostolic ministry. It shows that the "power-weakness" theme of all God's activity applies with special force to the Christian, who, through his intimate union with Christ, shares the death-life principle which leads both the body and the member through suffering to glory.

The study of Paul's teaching on suffering in his later captivity and pastoral epistles strongly corroborates the thesis that, in composing First Corinthians, Galatians, Romans and Second Corinthians, he was already in possession of the basic tenets of his full doctrine. The later epistles to Timothy and Titus, or to the Colossians and Ephesians make no essentially new contribution. Written in face of new developments and new problems in the community, they merely give fresh expression or application to doctrine which he has previously taught. This assertion is pointedly true of his teaching on Christian suffering, which is limited in extent and almost commonplace when compared with his treatment of this theme in Second Corinthians.

An apothegm in Second Timothy recalls substantially an earlier statement on the inevitability of suffering in Christian life. "All who want to live piously in Christ Jesus," Paul wrote to Timothy, "will suffer persecution" (3:12). Such struggle is represented as the consequence of the Christian's share in the life and power of Christ; for to live with Him means to die to all that is hostile to God. This principle, as applied to Baptism in Romans, is echoed in Colossians, where the sacramental death of Baptism is called "the circumcision of Christ" and consists in putting off the "body of flesh" through incorporation into Christ who died in His "body of flesh" to save us (Col. 2:11).

The consequent lifelong war against the flesh which faces every Christian is proposed anew in Colossians and Ephesians. This struggle, as we read in Second Timothy, is particularly acute in the lives of apostles. The power of Christ, however, can always be counted on to sustain loyalty and to strengthen patience. Endured in this spirit, suffering is a true favor from God. From the beginning of his ministry to its close, Paul saw in Christian trials a preparation for and a guarantee of heavenly reward. Near the moment of "being poured out in sacrifice," Paul wrote to Timothy: "I have fought the good fight, I have finished the course, I have kept the faith. For the rest, there is laid up for me a crown of justice, which the Lord, the just Judge, will give to me in that day; yet not to me only, but also to those who love his coming" (2 Tim. 4:7f.).

Thus the teaching of the captivity and pastoral epistles is thoroughly consonant with Paul's previous doctrine. There is one statement in the Epistle to the Colossians, however, which calls for special study.

Colossians 1:24 has a certain mysteriousness due in great part to the uncertain meaning of the phrase which

Paul employs. It reads: "I rejoice now in the sufferings I bear for your sake; and what is lacking of the sufferings of Christ I fill up in my flesh for his body, which is the Church."

In the first part of this verse, Paul declares that he rejoices in the sufferings which he bears for the Colossians. Here we meet elements which are frequent in Paul's writings. He has often mentioned the suffering he endured for his converts, and he has spoken of joy in suffering as a characteristic trait of all Christian spirituality.

The second part of the verse makes specific reference to his teaching on the Church as the body of Christ, for he expands the limited phrase "for your sake" into the wider one "for his body, which is the Church."

The fundamental question, however, centers in what Paul means by the phrase: "the sufferings of Christ." He has consistently spoken of the sufferings of *Christians*; never, except in four passages, has he joined the word to Christ's name (Col. 1:24; Rom. 8:17f.; 2 Cor. 1:4f.; 4:8, 10). Never, in fact, has any form of this expression been employed by Paul to refer to any aspect of Christ's earthly life. This is especially significant in view of the frequency with which he employs it to designate the sufferings of Christians. Finally, as we have seen, there is nothing in the immediate context or in the background of Pauline doctrine to urge the interpretation of "the sufferings of Christ" as referring primarily to a bond between Paul's trials and the historical sufferings of the Passion. Paul's phraseology finds full explanation in the light of his earlier doctrine on baptismal union with Christ. Because Christ is the Body in which the member lives and functions, His Spirit is the principle of all death-life and the prime mover in all Christian struggle. It is, above all, under this aspect that the trials of the Christian, and especially of an apostle, are the "sufferings of Christ."

There is nothing to indicate that Paul means anything else in Colossians 1:24. The immediate context of this verse is typically Pauline, while the verse itself seems to be inserted almost as a casual aside in the development of Paul's thought. It is not likely that a sentence, so incidental to his theme, will contain a new truth which he has never affirmed before. On the contrary, the verse bears marked resemblance to earlier texts and admits an interpretation thoroughly consonant with his usual doctrine. He has constantly asserted that the apostolate involves both a work to be done and sufferings to be borne if the body of Christ is to be built up and the life of Christ to be diffused to new members. But as there is a term to the development of the body of Christ, so there is a corresponding exigency to supply what is still lacking in apostolic labor and suffering. As a minister of the Gospel, Paul has received the commission to fulfill this need by preaching and by suffering. Such apostolic labor and trials are truly the "sufferings of Christ" because they are endured in His service and because His Spirit is the life-principle of His members.

A long search through the writings of St. Paul brings us now to the heart of his doctrine on Christian suffering. We read in his letter to the Philippians: ". . . that I may know him and power of his resurrection and the fellowship of his sufferings" (3:10).

The very word order of this verse parallels the events of his conversion, as set down in Acts. Its first element was his meeting with the risen Christ on the road to Damascus. This contact illumined his mind and aroused the first stirrings of new life; in very truth, Paul came "to know Christ in the power of his resurrection." But immediately after this experience he learned that suffering was to fill his life: "I will show him how much he must suffer for my name." His surrender to the risen Christ, although life-giving, involved also a share of suffering. In the story of his conversion, therefore, two elements are essential: vivifying contact with the Lord of glory and a declaration of the necessity of suffering. In the order of actual occurrence, the first preceded the second.

Paul's aim in Philippians, however, is not merely to summarize the incidents of his conversion. He is here writing an apologia for Christianity itself so that, although he speaks of his own conversion, he brings to light the excelling "gains" of which every Christian can boast. Paul understood well that his "I" is the "I" of every Christian and that the new life which he received through conversion is the same reality which every Christian possesses through Baptism. He speaks, moreover, of the benefits of life in Christ from the vantage point of rich experience and mature understanding.

It is clear from the climactic rise in the verses that Paul singles out the parousia-resurrection as the ultimate "gain" dominating all motives. ". . . that I may know him and the power of his resurrection and the fellowship of his sufferings: become like him in death, in the hope that somehow I may attain to the resurrection from the dead."

Hope for final union with Christ has been a theme throughout the whole epistle. To reach this union necessitates previous labor and suffering. Even the Jews, with their doctrine of the messianic tribulations, recognized that one attained to glory only through suffering. But how vastly different was the doctrine of Paul. For him, to attain the ultimate Christian reward, so eminently superior to Jewish resurrection, one had to live and to suffer in the Christian

way, so eminently superior to Jewish righteousness. The
"gain" of Christianity consisted not only in the excelling
end at which it aimed—resurrection in and with Christ—
but also in the excelling *way* whereby it reached that goal
—life in and with Christ. In Judaism men suffered in order
to be glorified; in Christianity men suffered *with Christ* in
order to be glorified *with Christ*.

Man enters on this way through conversion-baptism. At
that moment, the new member is united to the body of
Christ and receives the gift of the Spirit. The Spirit vivifies
what was dead by infusing the very life of the risen Christ
which will one day manifest its full vitality in the parousia-
resurrection. As with Paul on the way to Damascus, so too
with the Christian in Baptism, the first "gain" of conversion
is "to know Christ in the power of his resurrection."

But there is another essential "gain" which Paul describes
as "the fellowship of his sufferings." To urge his converts
to firmness in the faith, Paul reminds them that their suffering is a sign of salvation, for it is a gift of God like faith
itself. There is no question that he sees a strongly active
element in the suffering of which he speaks. For he has
previously described the activity of the Philippians as a
manly strife and immediately afterwards explains their
suffering with the parallel phrase, "engaged in the same
struggle."

"Fellowship of his sufferings," therefore, could be interpreted as referring to the Christian's share in the passion
of Christ. As we have already seen, however, Paul has
spoken so rarely of a parallelism between Christian suffering and the historical sufferings of Christ that it does not
seem likely he would highlight such a feature in this con-
densed statement of the essential elements of Christian life.
The reproduction in the Christian of the historical sufferings

of Christ, whether by mystical identity or by physical similarity, can hardly be called an essential or even primary element in Pauline doctrine.

On the other hand, the phrase, "fellowship of his sufferings," could refer to sufferings that are borne for Christ, in His cause. Undoubtedly, this element plays a role in Paul's thought. But to limit the content of the phrase to this meaning alone—that is, to a merely external bond between Christian suffering and Christ—does not accord with the demands of Pauline thought. Paul is here speaking of life in Christ and of the fullness of its "gains." He has just referred to the activity of the Holy Spirit which constitutes the "power of Christ's resurrection"; immediately afterwards he speaks of the conformity to Christ's death which leads to resurrection from the dead, a conformity which is effected by the Spirit of Christ working within the baptized. Both of these themes are related essentially to Paul's rich concept of life in Christ. It seems likely, therefore, that the intermediary phrase is also of the same nature.

This inference is wholly consonant with a truth that has emerged clearly from our review of Paul's doctrine: the truth, namely, that Christian suffering has deep theological roots in his teaching on union with Christ. This doctrine, as we have seen, supposes that every Christian receives at Baptism the efficacy of the salvific death and resurrection once accomplished in the body of Christ to which he is now united: "Do you not know that we who have been baptized into Christ have been baptized into His death?" (Rom. 6:3). This "gain" of Christian life may be viewed both as it exists in the first moment of conversion when it is simply life-with-Christ and death-with-Christ, and also as it exists in the lifelong process of preparation for the ultimate goal of parousia-resurrection. When Paul speaks of this second aspect, he always sees it as a process involving trial and suffering. For after Baptism the Christian must continue to live in the "flesh" and to deal with the "world," both of which form an ambient, hostile to the love of God and the life of the Spirit. If, therefore, the member of Christ is to live the risen life of the Savior, he must be crucified to the "world"; he must put to death the "deeds of the flesh." In a word, baptismal death with Christ must be renewed constantly throughout earthly life if one is finally to attain the ultimate goal of parousia-resurrection with Christ.

The "gain" of Paul's conversion, therefore, and of every Christian in Baptism, consisted not merely in momentary death with Christ, but in the fact that it inaugurated a life-long *state of death,* through the power of the Spirit, to the world, to the flesh, and to sin, both in his own life and in the lives of all whom he must gain for Christ. This Christian experience constitutes the *fellowship of his sufferings.*

This phrase means, undoubtedly, that such suffering is borne for Christ and is incurred in laboring for His cause. It means, too, that such suffering is supported in the spirit of His virtues. But, according to the rich Pauline concept, all this is true because the bond between Christian suffering and Christ Himself is rooted in the bond that unites body and member. Such suffering is truly "Christ's," because the love which impelled Him to die is the very same love which the Spirit infuses into His members so that they die daily to all that is opposed to God.

It is significant that Paul speaks here of "knowing the fellowship of his sufferings" rather than simply "knowing his sufferings." The word "fellowship" introduces into this phrase the spirit of the whole epistle. Throughout, he has shown himself vitally conscious of the part which all his fellow Christians play in working and suffering for the

Gospel; several times, in fact, he has used the word "fellowship" to express the close bond that unites them and to describe the share which the Philippians have contributed. Now, in 3:10, with graceful allusion to the part which his converts play, Paul speaks of his sufferings as a fellowship of His immense suffering. For truly his own daily experiences of "dying" formed but a share of the vast *sufferings of Christ* which all Christians, and especially apostolic laborers, must bear in order to bring the body of Christ to full measure.

"Fellowship in Christ's sufferings" is, therefore, a reality in all Christian living. If Paul here refers the phrase to himself, it is because every Christian can make the same boast and must follow the same example. For all life in Christ is vital with the activity of the Holy Spirit who daily renews in the members of Christ's body the love and obedience which inspired the Savior to undergo the passage of death. This experience involves every Christian in a crisscross of two levels—life in Christ and life in the flesh. Tension and struggle are inevitable. But always the resultant suffering is truly a share in the *sufferings of Christ*, for the glorious Savior claims as His own the sufferings which the dynamic presence of His Spirit occasions in His members.

CHAPTER 7 **THE SPIRIT OF CHRIST IN THE CHRISTIAN**

IN THIS DAY of giant strides toward unity, it pays to walk in the steps of Paul. Better than all others he has shown the way to break down barriers between Jew and Greek, slave and freeman, male and female.

His vision at the gates of Damascus changed the whole course of his life. The hardness of earth melted under the flame of heaven's mercy. Near-sighted eyes of flesh were blinded by light which illumined the whole world of spirit. In a moment this narrow-minded Jew, locked in insularity, heard walls crumbling around him and glimpsed a wide way opening before him.

To say that he saw Christ, the Lord of glory, is not enough. He saw Christ and His world-wide mission. Paul insisted on this. In each retelling of his conversion, he recalled the words which revealed the One living in many, the Savior at home in the hearts of men: "Saul, Saul, why dost thou persecute *me*? . . . I am Jesus whom thou art persecuting" (Acts 9:4).

Many years would pass before Paul understood the full

meaning of these words. Daily experience of life in the Christian community and constant struggle to safeguard its truth, prayerful pondering of God's promises to Israel and persevering meditation on Christ's own words—all this was needful to teach Paul how dynamically the Lord of glory is really living in every Christian.

His early epistles to the Thessalonians center attention on the glorious consummation of the second coming when all Christians shall come to live gloriously with the Lord. In these letters, however, Paul also intimates that his converts are already "in Christ Jesus." This phrase would become the very emblem of his fully developed thought. When at last he achieved mature understanding of the intimate bond between the risen Lord and the Christian upon earth, he still used this phrase to express his right insight: "You are in Christ Jesus" (1 Cor. 1:30).

These words are fundamental in understanding Paul's concept of life in the Church. Some have interpreted the formula in a grossly material way. They have spoken of a "mystical Christ," or a "pneumatic Christ"—something more extensive than the Savior himself, something like a "Christ-atmosphere" in which each Christian is suspended. Such imagery is completely foreign to Paul's thought. When he speaks of Christ, he has in mind only the real Jesus. When he speaks of the Christian "in Christ," he thinks only of an intimate bond of affection and dependence uniting two real persons.

Fully to appreciate his thought, we must understand the three elements which form the content of the simple statement, "You are in Christ Jesus."

The first element is the truth that Christ, rising from the dead, received dynamic power from his Father to become the "second Adam," the unique source of spiritual life for all men. Like Daniel's Son of Man incorporating the saints of Israel, he has received from the Ancient of Days unfathomable riches for all. God "has not spared even his own Son, but has delivered him for us all, how can he fail to grant us also all things with him?" (Rom. 8:32).

This truth involves a second and correlative element, the Christian's total dependence on Christ. Everything he is and has as a Christian he owes to the risen Savior who is Lord of all. Paul reminds the Corinthians of this total indebtedness: "You are in Christ Jesus, who has become for us God-given wisdom, and justice, and sanctification, and redemption; so that, just as it is written, 'Let him who takes pride, take pride in the Lord' " (1 Cor. 1:30f.).

It is this element which most pointedly underlies the phrase "You are in Christ Jesus." Just as Israel of old was to lean upon God and to trust completely in Him, so the new Israel must live in complete dependence on Jesus. In the "new creation," the risen Christ is the only source of all life and action. "So that henceforth we know no one according to the flesh," Paul writes. "If then any man is in Christ, he is a new creature: the former things have passed away; behold, they are made new!" (2 Cor. 5:16f.).

The total dependence binding the Christian to Christ finds perfect expression in a third element which points up the realism of Paul's thought. The Christian is one with Christ, intimately united to His body. To measure the exact meaning of this truth, we must remember that Paul was a Hebrew in all his thought-patterns. For him the body was not merely the neutral part of the Greek composite of body and soul. Paul the Semite knew no such dichotomy. Like every Hebrew, he regarded man as a perfect unity; the body was the whole man, a personalized and animated thing completely unified in its psychosomatic activity.

A Christian's dependence on Christ, therefore, meant

real union with the body-person of the Savior. Paul introduces this truth almost casually, in his treatment of a vexing problem at Corinth. There many were slipping back into old practices of impurity. Such sin was no mere fleshly indulgence. Prompted by desire for personality fulfilment, it involved the psychological and emotional union of a whole person with a whole person. Paul castigates this sin as infidelity, as a rupture of the only union which really counts. "Do you not know that your bodies are members of Christ? Shall I then take the members of Christ and make them members of a harlot?" (1 Cor. 6:15)·

Later Paul or his disciple introduces a more graceful comparison, likening the union of Christ and the Christian to the sacred intimacy of married life (Eph. 5:25-33). In both cases, however, his concept is alive with realism. The Christian united by Baptism to Christ and receiving from him all power and goodness becomes a living counterpart of Christ's own person: "For all you who have been baptized into Christ, have put on Christ. There is neither Jew nor Greek; there is neither slave nor freeman; there is neither male nor female. For you are all one in Christ Jesus" (Gal. 3:27f.).

It would be easy to treat these words as merely figurative language, if Paul the theologian had not put his finger on the deep, underlying reason for his realistic teaching on the Christian's intimate union with Christ.

At Baptism, he affirms, Christ shares with the man of faith the very Spirit who inspires and rules His own human life. The Spirit of Jesus becomes the Spirit of His follower. Christ and the Christian live and move under the impelling inspiration and empowering help of the same Holy Spirit of God. This is the whole burden of Paul's thought in Romans 8—a chapter which he has anticipated succinctly in a single sentence: "And because you are sons,

God has sent the Spirit of his Son, into our hearts, crying, 'Abba! Father!' " (Gal. 4:6).

For Paul, therefore, Christ is dynamically united to each baptized Christian as body-person to body-person through the power and guidance of His indwelling Spirit: "For in one Spirit we were all baptized into one body" (1 Cor. 12:13).

This theme of union with the body of Christ occurs frequently in the first letter to the Corinthians. Some have suggested that it means no more than the body-image of world unity prevalent in current Stoic philosophy. It is easily possible that Paul's emphasis on the body in this letter to Greek converts was due to the wide use of this image in the contemporary Greek world. Paul's concept, however, is rooted in a fact which the Stoic never dreamed of.

If he describes the Church as the "Body of Christ," it is primarily because he sees an intimate union between the body-person of Christ and the body-person of the Christian. He knew by experience the transforming influence of the Spirit of Christ at the moment of every Baptism. He was keenly aware, as Dr. Rawlinson has emphasized, that in the "breaking of bread" Christians renewed the faith-experience of Baptism to become more intimately united with the risen Christ. These facts, far more than a prevalent Greek terminology, prompted him to use the concept of body unity in solving the bristling problem which had arisen at Corinth.

Word had reached Paul that pride threatened the unity and harmony of the Corinthian church. Diversity of gifts had led many to despise the less favored or to resent the more gifted. For Paul this was a blatant denial of the real meaning of life in Christ.

To restore unity he had to reaffirm the total dependence

of every Christian upon Christ. He begins with the reminder that Christian faith itself is the gift of the Spirit: "No one can say 'Jesus is Lord!' except under the influence of the Holy Spirit" (1 Cor. 12:3). Spiritual life from its first confession of faith to its final experience of mystical insight into the mystery of Christ—all this is the gift of the Spirit.

Whatever good the Church possesses cannot be the fruit of merely human initiative or the achievement of merely human endeavor. Paul has intransigently ruled out the "wisdom of the wise" and the "cleverness of the clever" as possible sources of true Christian life (1 Cor. 1:19). He has insisted that the "wisdom of the world" is "foolishness" in comparison with the work of God. Genuine Christian life and action find their only source in the Spirit of Christ who shares the very life of the Savior with His followers.

Paul is insistent on this truth: "There are varieties of gifts, but the same Spirit. There are varieties of ministries, but the same Lord. There are many forms of work, but the same God, who works all things in all" (1 Cor. 12:4-6).

No one could deny that the Corinthian church was rich in the variety of its gifts. Christ's power was refracted, like the white light of the sun, into the multi-coloured beauty of divergent human graces. Paul's care is to emphasize that human personalities are idle prisms with no light to refract if they are not filled by the Spirit of Christ. Whatever gifts exist in the Church, therefore, "are the work of one and the same Spirit, who divides to everyone according as he will" (1 Cor. 12:11).

The Corinthians had overlooked yet another truth which would have saved them from pride and selfishness. They had forgotten what it means to live as a member of a body.

Paul, therefore, spells out his doctrine once more since it provides a compelling argument for unity. Christians must learn to work together and to respect one another because they form the one body of Christ. "For as the body is one and has many members, and all the members of the body, many as they are, form one body, so also is it with Christ" (1 Cor. 12:12).

This body-union of Christians in Christ is for Paul a first principle. It is the immediate and necessary effect of the two great Christian sacraments, Baptism and Eucharist. Paul leaves no doubt of this: "For in one Spirit we were all baptized into one body, whether Jews or Gentiles, whether slaves or free; and we were all given to drink of one Spirit" (1 Cor. 12:13).

Through the Spirit every Christian is bound as a member to the body-person of Christ, forming with Him the unity of a vital body, not the solidity of an unchanging monolith. This means that, like the human body itself, the body of Christ needs separate parts and members which function together in harmony and rhythm for the well-being of the whole body.

Paul develops this theme of unity in diversity through a succession of verses whose meaning no one can miss. He begins by affirming the obvious fact, "A body is not one member, but many" (1 Cor. 12:14). He exemplifies this by showing how the body needs each of its limbs and organs for integral life. Lest anyone mistake his point, he expresses it with unmistakable literalness: "If they were one member, where would the body be? But as it is, there are indeed many members, yet but one body" (1 Cor. 12:19f.).

This development does not yet touch the real problem of the Corinthian Church. Rivalry and jealousy did not arise from the variety of roles in the Church but from their seeming inequality. Some preened themselves on the possession of striking gifts; others boasted of an especially honorable office. In the life of the Church there seemed to be an aristocracy which many vaunted and many resented.

Paul finds a solution in the make-up of the human body itself. No matter how frail or unseemly an organ may be, it is often indispensable for the healthy functioning of the whole body (1 Cor. 12:21f.). What is more, a man's best efforts are often consumed in providing appropriate dress and ornament to hide an unseemly part of his body. Thus the whole man shows concern for every part of his body, especially for a part which is weak or suffering. God plans the same harmonious concern in the functioning of the Body of Christ. "God has so tempered the body together in due portion as to give more abundant honor where it was lacking; and there may be no division in the body, but that the members may have care for one another. And if one member suffers anything, all the members suffer with it, or if one member glories, all the members rejoice with it" (1 Cor. 12:24-26).

Paul applies this figure to the actual life of the community. He reveals the special point of what he has just said: "You are the body of Christ, member for member" (1 Cor. 12:27). Just as in the human body, so in the Church each member has a different role to play, a different function to fulfill. Yet all is under God's appointment, and each member has a vital role to play in the body of Christ. (cf. 1 Cor. 12:27-30).

Painstaking carefulness characterizes this whole development. With patient thoroughness Paul works out his theme of preserving unity in diversity. For once this im-

petuous thinker has put himself under severe restraint to
hold back the solution dearest to his heart. At last, however, his deepest thought bursts out: "Now", he cries, "I
will point out to you a way that surpasses all" (1 Cor.
12:31).

Love is the secret. Whatever unity there is in the Church
is the unity which comes from the Spirit's best gift to
Christ and to the Christian—*agape* (love). The love
which prompted Christ to assume every role, to perform
every function, to submit to every trial and suffering for
the salvation of men—this is the life principle which gives
meaning and nobility and dynamic power to every action
in the Church. Without this love the noblest gifts are
sterile; with it the least functions are dynamically powerful (*cf.* 1 Cor. 13:1-3).

For agape is the very love which Christ has. Paul's
description of it is a character profile of Him who gave
Himself totally to make every man one with Himself in
perfect unity. "Charity is patient, is kind; charity does not
envy, is not pretentious, is not puffed up, is not ambitious,
is not self-seeking, is not provoked; thinks no evil, does
not rejoice over wickedness, but rejoices with the truth;
bears with all things, believes all things, hopes all things,
endures all things" (1 Cor. 13:4-7).

This love is the one activity which endures after all of
God's other gifts in the Church have come to an end. It
alone passes over from the Church of earth to the glorious
kingdom of heaven. Let a man fulfill his role in the Church
with love, and his life will have eternal worth and meaning
(*cf.* 1 Cor. 13:8-13).

It is the best gift of the Spirit, the measure of all other
values: "And if I have prophecy and know all mysteries
and all knowledge, and if I have all faith so as to remove

mountains, yet do not have charity, I am nothing" (1 Cor. 13:2). It is the greatest of all God's gifts because it brings with it the perfect character traits of Christ himself: "The fruit of the Spirit is: charity, joy, peace, patience, kindness, goodness, fidelity, gentleness and self-control" (Gal. 5:22).

Paul wrote all this within the confined context of a particular problem at Corinth and within his own concept of the Church. He was not concerned with man's role in the world. For him human history spelled deterioration; the world was hastening to its dissolution (*cf.* Rom. 1:18-32). The only history he recognized was the new life which God was creating in and through the Church.

For the devout Jew, the Old Testament was a salvation history, the story of God at work bringing all to consummation in the kingdom of the Messiah. Nations had come and gone; they were nothing more than dry leaves of autumn; their history was a sweeping of dead branches into a bonfire. In Paul's perspective human history was no more than this. He was not interested in developing human culture or in advancing human wisdom (*cf.* 1 Cor. 1:18-31). The only thing which counted in his eyes was the life of Christ in His Church. This was God's work, the last stage of the only true "history." Whatever role man played, whatever function Paul spoke of, was an activity in the Church inspired by the Spirit to prepare for the end when Christ would "deliver up the kingdom to God the Father, after abolishing every kind of sovereignty, authority, and power" (1 Cor. 15:24).

But this wholly spiritual and predominantly eschatological perspective of Paul does not deprive his words of their directive power as principles. If anything, his limited perspective accentuates his principles, so that even today they are readily applicable to a changed situation.

For the outlook has changed. The world is not coming

to an end but is always with us. Horizons have expanded, and the Christian must live his life on compenetrating frontiers—in the body of Christ and in the world all around us. Today the Church is aware of her incarnational character in a way that Paul did not see. Had he glimpsed these vaster horizons, he might have failed to enunciate his guiding principles with the same sharpness and clarity. Ours would be the loss, for we need his principles now as never before.

Paul holds it as a first truth that whatever light shines, whatever power animates, whatever truth guides, is the beneficient action of Christ working through His Holy Spirit. This principle dissolves the walls of particularism which check the dynamic effort of Christ to enlighten and unify the world. For it inculcates a spirit of respect for every word of truth, for every good performance, for every healing purpose launched upon a weary world.

The divisions between Churches and nations are real. It will take a long while for walls to crumble. Barriers centuries in the making will not dissolve before mere human wish. Meanwhile, however, the Holy Spirit is doing His work in every group and in every man. The first step to unity, then, is to rejoice in His action wherever we find it.

This means not only approval but cooperation. Each new endeavor to forge the unity of nations, to secure the improvement of man's lot, to advance technological progress, to save what is authentically human, and to salvage the wreck which man has made of man—all this may well be prompted by God's own Spirit preparing the way for the union of all men in the body-person of Christ. A chauvinism which refuses to cooperate generously with the activity of other groups and other persons may impede the work and the purpose of the Spirit.

Quite as important for Paul was a second principle—

the diversity of the Spirit's action in the Church. Few have had such a keen sense of each man's special gift for building up the Body of Christ. He warned the Thessalonians, "Do not stifle the Spirit. Do not despise prophecies. But test all things; hold fast that which is good. Keep yourselves from every kind of evil" (1 Thess. 5:19-22). He it was, too, who urged the Corinthians, "There are other gifts of the Spirit at which you should aim also" (1 Cor. 14:1).

In the earthly life of the Savior every role and action had its own special value: now He spoke and again he acted; He rejoiced and was tempted; He prayed and preached; He suffered and died. Each facet of His human life was precious because all was under the lead and inspiration of the Spirit. For Paul the Spirit still manifests this same diversity in the Body of Christ which is the Church. Every gift, every spiritual talent, is something to be treasured and something to be used.

This principle calls for unfailing application in our own day. Each man has his own gift from God, his own role to play. The providence so clearly manifest in the distribution of gifts in the early Church is now just as much at work in the prudence which each man must exercise in making his own contribution to the world which is Christ's. Talents and aptitudes, desires and ambitions, background and social circumstance—all this is now the vehicle of God's direction in human life. A student's diligence in his studies and a professor's carefully prepared lecture, money-making plans and a genius for inventing gimmicks have as much a role to play in the salvation of the world as the gifts of teaching and exhorting, of administration and hospitality in the early Church. A politician at work to win an election, a research student tracing an intricate problem in history, can be as needful to the world as the "prophet" of the early community. The gifts are all still with us, even though we call them by other names.

The all-important thing is to see a job as a vocation, to see work as a contribution, to accept one's way of life, whether in the university or secondary school, whether in business or politics or the arts, as a role which one must fulfill to make the world more ready, even in the slightest way, to become the world of Christ.

This vision carries with it a tremendous responsibility. Only too often, however, the eye is blinded by fear and uncertainty, and the heart is torn by painful wonderment and an agonizing sense of ineptitude. The task seems so mammoth, and we have so little personal awareness of the Spirit Himself at work—in our life, in our activities, in our soul.

That is why we need the "best gift" which Paul singles out as the solution of the whole problem of men at work under the Spirit to build up the body of Christ.

Love is the way, and love is the meaning of it all. This is Paul's third principle.

A man might spend the whole of life trying in vain to make his contribution to the world; love will give his every effort a divine impact. He may seem merely to walk a treadmill; love bears his steps into every human heart. The best vision of faith may be but an invitation to the agony of failure. But love turns every agony on the cross into a cry of joy over the glorious resurrection of mankind.

Love—and the work will be done.

It must be so. For love means the presence of the Holy Spirit who is all-powerful in building up on earth the body of Christ.

CHAPTER 8 WITH CHRIST
AFTER DEATH

CATHOLIC thought today has registered its own emphasis in eschatology. The popular mind centers attention on the definitive judgment which launches the soul at death upon an eternity of joy or of anguish. In this frame of reference the apocalyptic events of the end-time claim little interest. For most people the general judgment is only consequential and secondary, a mere ratification of the preliminary decision which is far more important.

It may come as a surprise, then, to learn that the Christians of New Testament times did not share this outlook. Their preoccupation centered in the Parousia, in the apocalyptic return of Christ as Judge and Savior. The interest in the final restoration was so dominant that it tended to withdraw attention from the immediate aftermath of death.

This outlook of the early Church was the consequence of its biblical and Jewish background. Christ and the Judeo-Christian community made their own the eschatology which Hebrew thought had formulated after the long and intricate processes of its development. Even now it is difficult to trace the devious course which led from the early belief in collective and worldly retribution to the post-exilic hope of other-worldly reward both for the collected people of God and for the individual. The course of development was so complex that the Jews never produced a universally accepted eschatology. We cannot speak of a Jewish *dogma* of retribution after death even in our Lord's own day. The Sadducees, with no belief in reward after death, could and did attain to the highest positions in church and state.

The theology of the Pharisees, however, dominated the scene. These respected leaders taught the doctrine of an apocalyptic end-time and the bodily resurrection of the just as it is enunciated in the biblical books of Daniel and Second Machabees or in non-biblical books like Enoch or the Psalms of Solomon. As G. F. Moore has well noted, the thesis of the Pharisees was the natural consequence of God's revelation: "On the premises of Scripture, the only logical way in which the Jews could conceive the fulfillment of God's promises to the righteous was that they should live again upon earth in the golden age to come and share in the salvation of Israel. The resurrection seems, indeed, so necessarily the consequence of the whole teaching of Scripture concerning the salvation of the righteous and their great reward that it is not strange that the Pharisees found it explicit or by intimation in all parts of their Bible" (*Judaism,* II, 313-314).

Christ accepted this doctrine and made it His own, thus giving certainty to the essential feature of final retribution. His synthesis of the highest developments in Old Testament revelation stands as a basic assumption in all New Testament thought.

The essential features of the doctrine of Christ and the Pharisees bring to the fore the three elements which remained constant in Hebrew thought on retribution despite the many changes which preceded its final formulation. For in all stages of its development this doctrine shows three characteristics which are inherent in biblical thought. These dominant elements must be kept in mind if we are to understand the teaching and spirit of our early Christian sources.

First of all, every biblical theory of retribution provides for man as an animated and personalized body and not as a dichotomy of body and soul as in the Greek system. Whether in the early concept of reward and punishment on this earth or in the late development of retribution in an after-life, the *whole* man is always involved. Biblical man lives always as an animated body, and so as a body he must be rewarded. No people ever had so keen a sense of man's psychosomatic unity as did the Semites.

Secondly, every Hebrew theory of retribution looks primarily to the social group. With historical origins in a close-knit tribal society and with divine origin in a covenant between God and the People, Israel never lost sight of the fact that it must live as a people. Even when the individual emerges in the theology of Jeremia and Ezechiel, the devout Israelite finds his fulfillment and mission in the nation's destiny to glorify God as a corporate personality (*cf.* Jer. 31:29-34; Ez. 18). A markedly personal note characterizes the postexilic piety of the *anawim;* in their prayer, however, they remain always aware of membership in the *Qehal Yahweh.* This corporate consciousness of Israel is the very context in which they lived. It is the background of their piety and the support of their confidence.

The Bible, therefore, is alien to the subjectivism and

atomistic individualism of our age. The hopes of the individual may be fired with the flame of his own personality; their fulfillment always includes the collectivity. Whether retribution is on this earth or in a world to come, whether reward involves the whole nation or only the just, Hebrew thought always centers in the social group.

Thirdly, every theory of retribution always gives first place to God and His glory. In the beginning men were content to die after a long and blessed life on earth and to pass into the namelessness of Sheol, happy in the thought that their people would continue to dwell on the land and to glorify God. When this confidence was shattered by the nation's infidelity, men had to seek another theory of retribution to safeguard God's glory. His honor was one of the motives which drove Israel from one theory to another until at last it reached the perfect eschatological dream which envisioned endless glory for God through endless praise offered by the risen just.

These three themes dominated the retribution thesis of the Pharisees. The end-time would bring full reward in the presence of God to the resurrected nation and to the righteous individual. The nation of the just would thus glorify God forever. This belief rings through the confession of faith uttered before Antiochus by the Machabee martyrs (2 Mach. 7:9ff.).

Late Hebrew thought knew also that reward and punishment begin in some way immediately after death. The justice of God and the survival of man required this. In the literature, written during the gap of time between the Old and New Testament, Sheol ceased to be merely an abode of the dead, without distinction in reward and punishment. It became instead a provisory stage where the dead anticipate their future lot. One part of this rest-ing-place is called Paradise, for there the just enjoy felicity; another part, called Gehenna, is a place of punishment for the wicked.

This late development in Jewish eschatology lacks the clearness and certainty of the Pharisee thesis on retribution at the end-time. The Hebrew mind, with its compelling sense of man's unity, found it difficult to conceive of reward and suffering for a disembodied spirit. Whatever is positive in this picture of man's lot during the interim period between the Old and New Testament seems to borrow shape, tone, and color from the picture of the final drama.

Christ made His own the doctrine of the Pharisees on the end-time, sharpening its focus and stabilizing its certainty through His own teaching and that of His apostles. We turn to the Gospels first; though they are among the latest compositions of the early Christian Church they are true to the teaching and emphases of Jesus Himself.

During His earthly life Christ was engaged in building a bridge between the worlds of the Old and New Covenants. It was His task to herald the fulfillment of Old Testament hopes and to manifest Himself as the full and perfect embodiment of all that God had promised. Men had to see in Him the eminent source of all salvation and the consummation of age-long expectancies.

He made clear enough that His kingdom would enjoy moments of growth and would suffer moments of waning. At the same time, however, He did look forward to playing a special role in the future, eschatological consummation. Christ did not limit His vision to a "realized eschatology"—as though every hope had already been "realized" in His earthly life and resurrection.

Christ spoke also of the immediate aftermath of death, making his own the Pharisee doctrine on the interim period.

It is to Luke that we are indebted for the memory of these words of Jesus. This is significant. Luke the Greek, writing for Greeks, takes care to record the doctrine which matches their interest in the fate of man when life on earth comes to an end.

To Luke we owe Christ's parable of Dives and Lazarus (16:19-31). Christ speaks here of reward and punishment after death, painting His picture as the Pharisees did with the colors of final retribution, yet scaling down the perspective to accord with the interim period. The picture was a common one; in renewing it and making it His own, Christ confirmed belief in reward and punishment following immediately upon death.

Luke makes a more important contribution in recording Jesus' word to the thief on the cross: "This day thou shalt be with me in Paradise" (23:43). This promise serves as a guide to our own doctrine on the interim period. Jewish thought had focused attention on a place of bliss described in terms of earthly pleasure—the food of life, living water, shade, rest, light; this they called Paradise. In His messianic proclamation from the cross, Jesus effects a transition from the Jewish hope of Paradise to the Christian hope of union with Christ: "You shall be *with me.*" This word makes clear that even immediately after death the righteous man enjoys the companionship of the king of the messianic realm.

We are indebted to Luke also for the revealing incident of Stephen's death. The account in Acts 7:54-60 makes clear that even though the thought of the Parousia dominated the mind of the early Christian writers, they possessed at the same time a concept of union with Christ at death. As L. Cerfaux points out, it is the Christ of the Parousia whom Stephen beholds. The circumstances of the vision, however, indicate that His presence is meaningful here and now. Christ does not "sit" at the right hand of the Father in the role of judge. Instead he "stands" in an attitude of expectant welcome. The words which Stephen utters, "Lord, receive my spirit," are the very words which Jesus used to surrender Himself into the bosom of His Father (Lk. 23:46). "With these words he [Stephen] fell asleep." The real meaning of this cliché, so frequent in Jewish literature, must be gleaned from the context. There is no question of "awakening" only at the final resurrection. Even at the moment of death Stephen lives in some way "with Christ."

St. Paul hardly made any real advance beyond these contributions of St. Luke. In his eschatology as in his anthropology he is a Pharisee of the Pharisees; he knows and accepts what is best in Jewish thought. There is great value, however, in studying his contribution. As the theologian of the Church he saw clearly what Christianity had done to sharpen the focus of Old Testament revelation and to illumine it with the light of Christ. Secondly, his letters are the earliest writings of the New Testament period, not written like the Gospels to reproduce the words and teachings of Jesus, but to show the full mind of the Church in Paul's own day. In reading his epistles, therefore, we come to grips with flesh and blood Christianity between 50 and 60 A.D.—with its attitudes and interests.

In these letters the Parousia comes frequently to the fore, not only in the beginning of his ministry (it is the whole burden of Thessalonians) but also at its close. In dying Paul looks forward to "that day": "There is laid up for me a crown of justice which the Lord, the just Judge, will give to me in that day; yet not only to me, but also to all those who love His coming" (2 Tim. 4:8).

In the captivity epistles his attention to the mystery of Christ leads him to concentrate on anticipated eschatology; through the *arrabon* (pledge) of the indwelling Spirit (Eph. 1:14) the Christian has already begun his future life. If anything, however, this foretaste serves to whet the desire for that day when, through resurrection, the whole man shall be with the Lord.

This prospect of a rich personal experience provides only a partial reason for the magnetism of the Parousia. The last day drew the mind of Paul much more because it represented the salvation of the whole body of Christ for the glory of the Father. For Paul, the Hebrew, salvation had to include the note of solidarity and further the glory of God. For Paul, the Christian, this meant the resurrection of the whole body of Christ for the glory of the Father. . . . "Then comes the end, when he delivers the kingdom to God the Father. . . . And when all things are made subject to him, then the Son himself will also be made subject to him who subjected all things to him, that God may be all in all" (1 Cor. 15:24, 28).

In Paul's judgment nothing could compare with the final consummation. For up until the Parousia death would reign; and for Paul death is not a mere biological fact but a tyranny, a penalty for man's offense which lay heavy not only upon the living but also in some way even upon the dead. The symbol and effect of sin, death was a power hostile to God which would continue to blight humanity even until the very end: "The last enemy to be destroyed will be death" (1 Cor. 15:26). Paul's lack of interest in the immediate aftermath of death and his yearning for the Parousia make clear that in his judgment even those who have died in the Lord still lack something.

In this regard it is significant that when the Thessalonians mourn their dead the Apostle does not comfort them with the reminder of a consummation in glory already achieved. He is content simply to point out that the living will have no advantage over the dead at the time of the Parousia. He says nothing more than this to reconcile his readers to the fate of those who have already died. For Paul the Hebrew, death stripping man of his body, stood in open hostility to the full consummation of God's glory and man's definitive salvation.

This attitude is fundamentally biblical and Hebrew. Paul's yearning for the Parousia echoes the hope of the author of Daniel for the total messianic victory over sin (*cf*. Dan. 9:24-25). The Apostle shares fully the ardent longing of the Prophet who looked beyond the "seventy weeks" to the definitive defeat of all evil and the total realization of all good.

There is, however, another essential element in Paul's teaching, and this is formally Christian. It is this aspect of his doctrine which illumines death with truly Christian light.

Through an act of supreme generosity Christ has made Himself one with the human solidarity which lies under the burden of sin and death. As a man, incorporating in Himself all that is human, He went through death in order to change the whole meaning of death. On Calvary He faced all the horrors of a death which sin had made terrible. He endured the experience dreaded by every man as God's worst punishment, and thus He Himself underwent God's judgment on the fallen human race.

It was precisely by this act that Christ took the bitter sting out of death (*cf*. 1 Cor. 15:56f.). Because He was God's own Son, death *had* to be for Him the doorway to life, the return to the bosom of His Father. Previously death was the consummation of man's separation from God; in

Christ it became the way of God. Previously it was the symbol of sin separating man forever from the living God. In Christ it became the supreme manifestation of loving obedience which promised immediate access to God.

Such a death, the death of God's own Son beloved by the Father and totally devoted to the Father, contained a compelling right to glorious risen life with the Father. "He became obedient unto death, even to death on a cross. *Therefore* God has exalted him" (Phil. 2:8f.). The connective "therefore" marks the consequence not of mere promise but of inherent necessity. Resurrection was contained in the very nature of this death as the life of the flower is contained in the seed.

For Paul nothing could be more definitive than the death-resurrection of Christ. His passage from life in this world broke the tie which bound him to "flesh," the solidarity of earthly existence, with its inherent qualities of weakness, mortality and distance from God. Death swept Him out beyond everything which bore the blight of life upon earth—the flesh and the law, sin and suffering, earthly weakness and death itself. Through resurrection He began an entirely new life in which he could give full play to the love and power which is His as messianic Son of God: "We know that Christ, once raised from the dead, is never to die again: he is no longer under the dominion of death. For in dying as He died, He died to sin, once for all, and in living as He lived, He lives to God" (Rom. 6:9f.).

There is another factor equally essential to Paul's thought. The death-resurrection of Christ is of benefit not only to Himself but to all Christians. He died and rose again as a corporate personality, bearing all men in Himself to the Father. The Hebrew conception of corporate personality underlies Paul's whole concept of the role of Christ. Like Adam, Christ embodies and represents all men; He is the new Adam (*cf.* 1 Cor. 15:22, 45-49). Through the law of solidarity, therefore, His death and resurrection are efficacious for all: "We have come to the conclusion that, since one died for all, therefore all died" (2 Cor. 5:14). The experience of Christ, like the life in Adam, has power to extend and to renew itself in every man. That is why Paul can write in the name of every Christian: "With Christ I am nailed to the cross. It is now no longer I that live, but Christ lives in me" (Gal. 2:20).

Paul is not speaking of mere external imitation—"As Christ . . . so the Christian." His thought rests not on the level of external concomitance but on the deeper level of organic functioning. He speaks of the experience which he describes as life "in Christ Jesus."

In the Pauline vocabulary this phrase means a real and psychosomatic union between Christ and the Christian. Through Baptism the neophyte is so united to the risen body-person of the Savior that he shares the very life of Christ and becomes capable of extending the influence of His personality: "All you who have been baptized into Christ have put on Christ. There is neither Jew nor Greek; there is neither slave nor freeman; there is neither male nor female. For you are all one in Christ Jesus" (Gal. 3:27).

This union is both real and dynamic, bringing a vital share in the redemptive mysteries of Christ's own death and resurrection. What Christ has done in His body in dying on the cross and in rising from the dead is shared and reproduced in the Christian. The union between them is as exclusive and communicative as that of man and wife. This truth comes to clearest expression in Romans 7:4: "Therefore, my brethren, you have died to the law by becoming identified with the body of Christ, and accordingly you have found another [Husband] in him who rose from the dead, so that we may bear fruit for God."

The Christian does not merely assent psychologically to the redemptive activity of Christ, as some would hold. If that were the case, Calvary would be nothing more than another Sinai, and our justice would no longer be the gift of Christ but the wages of our own tedious human effort which always fails. To this latter suggestion Paul would have only one answer—*me genoito! Certainly not!* It repeats the fundamental error of the Judeo-Christians which Paul strove against throughout his ministry. He himself knows no other way of justice except that which he describes in Philippians 3:8-10: "I count [all things] as dung that I may gain Christ and be found in him, not having a justice of my own, which is from the Law, but that which is from faith in Christ . . . so that I may know him and the power of his resurrection and the fellowship of his sufferings."

All this becomes possible through the gift of the Spirit which the Christian receives when he is united to the body-person of Christ in Baptism. For the Spirit renews in the member of Christ the very death which the Savior died on the cross (death to the flesh and to sin); at the same time He vitalizes the Christian with the very life which Christ Himself now lives in glory. This share is so real that Paul does not hesitate to write: "We were buried with him by means of baptism into death, in order that, just as Christ has arisen from the dead through the glory of the Father, so we also may walk in newness of life" (Rom. 6:4).

This sharing in the mysteries of Christ is real yet not static. All during his days upon earth man must live *en Christo* (in Christ) while at the same time continuing his human life *en sarki* (in the flesh). The criss-cross of these two levels leads inevitably to tension and contradiction. Man is constantly drawn to assume again the "mind of flesh" (Rom. 8:5) which represents primarily a denial of man's dependence on God and a proud confidence in himself. For St. Paul, therefore, *sarx* implies much more than our English word *flesh; sarx* is man with all his faculties in rebellion against God. To react against this the Christian must often renew his baptismal death to sin and to *sarx* (*cf.* Rom. 6:12ff.).

Life with God, too, must know its constant deepening and increase. If the Christian has "put on" Christ at Baptism, he must ever continue to "put Him on" more and more throughout the course of his life upon earth. The mystery of Christ's resurrection once shared in is to be lived always more intensely. Christian life, therefore, knows a fundamental law of growth. The conformity to Christ which gives new shape and new vitality to the whole personality at Baptism is to grow constantly until at last it becomes perfect conformity through the Parousia-resurrection.

It is unfortunate that Paul's words on bodily resurrection in 1 Corinthians 15 have so often been considered apart from the consistent doctrine of the rest of his epistles. This has led to the mistaken notion that the final change will have in it something quasi-magical. Many indeed think of resurrection only as a physical resuscitation. They have overlooked Paul's words on the bond between resurrection and the indwelling Holy Spirit (Rom. 8:11). This Spirit is always at work preparing the Christian for the Parousia by perfecting his likeness to Christ. The glorious moment of bodily resurrection, therefore, is but the last and consummate stage of that conformation to Christ which has been going on all during life.

We are now in a position to estimate the full Pauline perspective on death and the Parousia. As a Jew and as a Christian he could not think of man's perfect salvation except in terms of the full glory of God, the full redemption of the solidarity, the full conformity of all men to Christ through the Parousia-resurrection. Obviously, therefore, his best thoughts always rested on the end-time of perfect consummation. Whatever took place before that was simply the development of man's first conformation to Christ through Baptism.

Père Feuillet has pointed out what is essential in this perspective: "Paul is interested above all in two crucial moments of our participation in the risen life of Christ: baptism which inaugurates this sharing and the Parousia which consummates it. Baptism makes us one with Christ in His death and resurrection; the glorious Parousia places the final seal on our conformity to Him. All that takes place between these two moments does not establish any really new relation to Jesus."

Physical death, therefore, claims no special attention in Paul's letters. In his eyes it does not bring that full life with God which only the *total* man can know. For this, resurrection is necessary, the resurrection of the individual and of the people of God. Death, therefore, marks only one more moment in the progressive conformation to Christ which is life's whole purpose.

He conceives of it only in the line of the progressive mortification of *sarx* which began at Baptism. Paul envisages all Christian existence as a death realized in principle on Calvary, commenced in fact for each Christian at Baptism, continued all through life, and completed by death "in Christ" at the term of one's earthly existence.

Death, therefore, is significant in Paul's mind not because it marks the consummation of entry into a new solidarity (only the Parousia could do that) but because it marks for the Christian the dissolution of the old solidarity of *sarx*. Even this significance, however, must be qualified. The dissolution is only partial; for the solidarity of the *sarx* is bound up with "this age" rather than with this earth. Even those who have died in Christ must still await the "redemption of the body" and the restoration of all things.

We cannot say, however, that Paul was indifferent to the experience of death. He spoke of it twice, and both times with an awareness that death is a blessing.

In Philippians 1:21-23 the Apostle, faced with martyrdom, expresses his longing for death and speaks of it as "a gain." "For to me to live is Christ and to die is gain. But if to live in the flesh is my lot, this means for me fruitful labor, and I do not know which to choose. Indeed I am hard pressed from both sides—desiring to depart and to be with Christ, a lot by far the better; yet to stay on in the flesh is necessary for your sake."

The most obvious remark one can make on these words is to note that were it a question of choice between life and the Parousia, instead of between life and death, Paul would not have experienced this uncertainty in making a choice.

In the present instance he inclines towards death. His reasons appear in the very words he employs. He sees death as a departure from the world of *sarx* and therefore the last stage in his baptismal death to sin and weakness. This means conversely an intensification of his life "with Christ." From now on he would walk uninterruptedly in that "newness of life" which has been his since Baptism. Death, therefore, is a true "gain" rendering definitive his baptismal death with Christ and intensifying his baptismal life with Christ.

The fact remains, however, that death is not the Parousia. It affects only Paul and not the solidarity. It brings the dissolution of *sarx* for Paul but not for the world. It lends new intensity to his personal life with Christ; but it does not bring life to the *whole* man. Death therefore, leaves much to be desired. And so, apart from this single fervent wish here, Paul centers his attention throughout the rest of this epistle on the Parousia.

This same spirit pervades Paul's second word on death— in 2 Corinthians 5:1-10. In this passage, moreover, he makes explicit the perspective which governs all his thinking. He begins with the mention of resurrection and ends with the reminder of judgment. The Parousia is always to the fore in his thought.

He is aware, though, that life has its immediate term in death when man leaves his body "to be at home with the Lord." Interpreted in the light of Paul's constant and fervent devotion to Christ this phrase has overtones of a rich personal companionship, which becomes all the more constant once *sarx* is laid aside.

To lay aside *sarx,* however, means to lay aside the body also. This prospect fills him with dismay. He frankly confesses that it takes courage to face this ordeal, for "to be unclothed" ruptures the securities of life as man knows it; death even at its best is an exile.

Once more Paul has sketched his scale of values. No matter what death may achieve in intensifying life with the Lord, it cannot match the full and rich consummation of the Parousia.

It is now clear that early Christian thought laid little emphasis on death and its immediate aftermath; interest centered chiefly in Parousia. It was the task of later theology to illumine the interim period between death and final consummation. This it did by focusing the light of precise philosophy on the data of revelation to formulate a full thesis on the beatitude of the soul immediately after death.

Unfortunately, the modern mind (the product of nineteenth century subjectivism and individualism) has so concentrated on the "salvation of the soul" at death that it no longer adjusts easily to the complementary perspective of the Parousia.

The vision of the early Church, however, is the very perspective most needed in our day. The salvation of all men and the glorification of the total man through resurrection are divine answers to a Communism which glorifies the collectivity and looks upon man above all as an animated body.

The salvation of the body corporate and the renewal of family ties before the Father on the last day provide a living hope which gives moment and meaning to our present ecumenical efforts.

The ultimate glory destined by God for the whole world is one of the best incentives to true Christian humanism. It is in the light of the Parousia that men come to understand best of all their duty to develop the world's resources, to foster men's talents, to lift human life from an inferior to a higher level. This is not merely a matter of social obligation or of civic pride; it is rather the working out of God's plan for the consummation of all things at the Parousia. For what will this final consummation mean except that once more the whole world which God has created will come completely under the control of Christ, Christ completely under His Father, giving into His hands the family and the Kingdom which He Himself has perfected.

CHAPTER 9 THE CHURCH
IN THE BIBLE

BIBLICAL scholars today are coming to see that the Church
has deep roots in the soil of the New Testament. To
many this may seem like the discovery of a truism. It is
rather a significant advance on the level of scholarship.

It was a previous fashion in some circles to treat the
Church as a foundling fathered by an ingenious primitive
community and laid on the doorstep of an unsuspecting
Christ. For Adolph Harnack the gospel was set foursquare
within the highly personal framework of God the Father,
His Providence, man's sonship, and the infinite worth of
the human soul. There was little room even for Christ in a
Gospel like that—much less for the Church. For Albert
Schweitzer Jesus' message centered in the imminent breakthrough of the heavenly kingdom by a divine coup d'état.
So, too, most other liberal scholars in the first quarter of
the present century found it difficult to ascribe to Jesus
of Galilee any idea of founding a Church.

Today, however, a change is notable. As Anton Fridrich-
sen has observed, "The discovery of the Church's role in

early Christianity is the greatest event within exegetical science in our generation." This is due in great part to the influence of the German form-criticism school. Scholars like Rudolph Bultmann and Martin Dibelius have so emphasized the creative power of the primitive apostolic community, that unwittingly they have made it difficult to accept their parallel thesis on the Church's spontaneous origin. An anonymous source for such a dynamic group as the early Christian community constitutes a vexing problem.

The disciples of Bultmann, therefore, are coming to see why their master has always shown signs of embarrassment when asked to explain the community itself. The primitive Church is a total anomaly unless one accepts its claim to intimate dependence on the person and ministry of Jesus. It is not surprising, then, that the recent works of Gunther Bornkamm and Harald Riesenfeld show the pendulum swinging back to center.

This return is inevitable. The Church looms so large and clear in the apostolic writings that it provides its own best proof of foundations which are solid and deep. When the eminent Pauline scholar Heinrich Schlier became a Catholic a few years ago, he wrote, "The insights which led me into the Church developed for me gradually, through my constant appraisal of the New Testament . . . They furnished me with reasons so powerful that I felt myself impelled and commanded to go off into that strange land in which my real home seemed to lie."

This is the confidence which every Catholic must possess. They must share Schlier's conviction that the image of the Church is so clear and consistent in the apostolic writings that this very image offers perennial proof of deep roots in the earthly life of Jesus.

This does not mean that we are to search the Scripture

for anachronisms. The Church is not monolithic; it is living. It has grown from a seedling to a world-wide organization, with a viability which permits adjustment to changing times and places. In the beginning it was a family where everyone knew everyone else, where Peter was a brother among brothers, and where those who had lived with Jesus and spoken with the risen Lord enjoyed prestige and authority everywhere. To seek identity between our local bishops and the "episcopoi" of Acts is to seek an anachronism. To look for what is Roman in Peter and to try to square the current pope with the lean fisherman of Galilee—this is like trying to fit the Roman office of the Passionist Generalate into the little hut where St. Paul of the Cross founded the Congregation in the eighteenth century.

It is not our purpose to search the apostolic writings for anachronisms which we shall never find there. What we are looking for are the basic elements of the Church's organization, the rationale of its disciplinary activity, and the pre-eminent source of its divine life and teaching.

Let us start at the beginning. Something happened at Pentecost—just as something happened at Sinai—to bring new people into being. Looking back years later St. Luke illumines the full significance of the event by developing in a highly literary form all the involvements of the coming of the Spirit. His midrashic description of the "tongues of fire," his rich use of the Old Testament prophecies in the Petrine discourse—all this emphasizes the truth that on Pentecost itself the followers of Jesus knew clearly that they had received from Him God's own Spirit. The risen Savior, therefore, was truly the messianic Son of God (*cf.* Acts 13:33) and they His messianic community.

This faith of Pentecost needs no proof. Though the

opening chapters of Acts owe much to the insights of Luke
and to his power of evoking impressions through a literary
use of rabbinical and scriptural themes, this section shows
also a consistent fidelity to the spirit and contents of its
source material. Whatever may have been the penetrating
power of his own developed theology Luke often presents
the thoughts of Peter and Stephen just as they thought them
in that first burst of Pentecostal light.

There is the telltale mark of primitive Christian thinking
in Peter's words when, with full conviction, he announces
the ringing challenge: "Let all the house of Israel know
most assuredly that God has made both Lord and Christ,
this Jesus whom you crucified" (Acts 2:36). When this
statement is brought next to later Pauline theology with its
more careful precision, we almost suspect an adoptionist
color to Peter's formulary. Luke, however, lets it stand,
even though it *sounds* so close to the heretical position that
Christ was not the consubstantial, but only the adoptive Son
of God. This same spirit of originality flavors Stephen's discourse in Acts 7. For this witness to the faith, the risen
Christ is everything while His passion and death are crucial
problems calling for apology. The substance of the sermon,
therefore, comes from the first days of Christianity, from
a level which was not yet enlightened by Paul's profound
insight into the real efficacy of Christ's death.

One truth especially emerges from these first pages of
Acts. The followers of Jesus believed that the "last day"
promised by the prophets had come. He whom they had
seen risen from the dead had Himself given them the Spirit
of God. He, therefore, was the Messiah; and they were the
messianic community.

Their life flowed along smoothly in the channels of
Jewry because they looked on themselves as its perfect
fulfillment. They felt no sharp cleavage with their own

people, since they were simply enjoying the privileges planned for all in Israel who would believe. When after the Resurrection they chose Matthias to fill out the number of the Twelve Apostles, they had in mind that judgment over the twelve tribes which the "last days" would bring. Now that this time had come they recognized themselves as the perfect Israel (Acts 3:24ff.). Their sense of having arrived filled these first days with a peace and overflowing joy which left a deep impression on their fellow-Jews (Acts 2:46f.).

Their belief that Jesus had risen from the dead as the messianic Son of God was bound to bring clashes, especially with the Sadducees (Acts 4:1-22; 5:17ff). Jesus as dead Messiah, however, did not create the same problem as Jesus the living reformer. Whatever tensions existed were not sufficient to cause a full rift; conflicts could be smoothed over in the same way in which Pharisees and Sadducees agreed to disagree over resurrection and life after death and the number of inspired books. We can speak, therefore, of a true continuity between Jewry and the primitive community. Just as Jesus had found place in the life of His people, so the followers of Jesus sensed no compelling reason in the Pentecostal experience to break with their background. They had simply entered upon the age for which Israel had always yearned.

There was, however, something dynamically new among Jesus' followers. Their attraction was that of vital youth. All around them was the shadow of aging hope; they, however, possessed the glorious substance of hope and the newness of life which only the Messiah could give. Jewry was powerless with the weakness of flesh; the community was strong with the vigor of the Spirit. Many elements of their life, therefore, made them different from their fellow Jews.

First of all, their preaching (the *kerygma*) set them

apart. Their one message to all men was the startling truth that the crucified Jesus had risen from the dead and had bestowed the messianic gift par excellence, the Holy Spirit (*cf.* Acts 2:29-36; 3:12-16). This made Him truly Messiah and Lord, the only source of salvation for all men (*cf.* Acts 4:8-12; 5:29-32). For those who accepted this truth there was always further instruction drawn not from Jewry but from Jesus. This was known as the "teaching [*didaché*] of the apostles" (Acts 2:42).

This brings to light a second distinctive characteristic of the new community. It was no longer the doctors of the Law or the Jewish leaders who taught and directed this group but rather the followers of Jesus who were in a special way the qualified "witnesses of His resurrection" (Acts 1:22; 5:32). The Twelve were now the acknowledged leaders, the chosen chiefs who spoke for the community and suffered for it and proclaimed intransigently all that it stood for.

The distinctiveness of the community was emphasized by a third special mark, its rite of initiation and its central mystery, "the breaking of bread." Even a circumcised Jew could not belong to this new group unless he professed faith in Jesus as the messianic Son of God and accepted Baptism which resembled the rite of heathen admission into the fold of Israel (Acts 2:38). Continuance in the community meant frequent sacramental contact with the Messiah Lord through the "bread" which He had provided. This was the one mystery which the community kept for itself as its special treasure and as the foretaste of the Lord's imminent return (the Parousia). For though the followers of Christ prayed in the Temple, they "broke bread" in their own homes (Acts 2:42, 46). While awaiting the glorious return of the Messiah Lord they found strength and joy in the

Bread which was Himself. This was what held them together; sharing in the body of Christ they became themselves that Body which is the Church (*cf.* 1 Cor. 10:16f.).

For the primitive community Christ was all in all. The
belief of all centered in Him (*cf.* Rom. 10:9f.); their leaders
were men chosen by Him; their very worship meant a
sharing in the mystery of His body and blood. Now they
awaited anxiously the days of refreshment, the Parousia,
when their judge and king would return to them in glory
that they might rejoice with Him forever (Acts 3:20).
They had much yet to learn of God's plan.

The next move was precipitated by the Hellenist Christians. As Oscar Cullmann has shown, these Greek-speaking
Jews had always irritated the homelanders by their disdain
for the physical elements of Israel's worship. Living in the
Diaspora they had found God away from the Temple and
had worshipped Him with a spiritual devotedness which
spurned the smell of blood and burning flesh. In coming to
know Jesus these Hellenists found the way of spiritual
worship wide open to them in the "Temple not made by
hands." When Stephen the Hellenist, therefore, spoke of
Jesus, his hearers had ears only for that irritating sentence
which echoed the old anti-Temple polemic: "Solomon built
him a house; yet not in houses made by hands does the
Most High dwell" (Acts 7:47f.).

That sentence was the signal for persecution. If the Jews
could tolerate within their own fold men who followed
Jesus as the Messiah, they could not stomach fellow-Jews
who cast aspersion on the most sacred element of Jewish
worship. And so "a great persecution broke out on that
day against the Church in Jerusalem" (Acts 8:1). Yet
not against all the Church. Persecution left the Galilean
apostles untouched. Only Stephen the Hellenist was mar-

tyred; and only the Hellenist Christians were driven from their Jerusalem home.

This was a stroke of Providence. By it the Church was forced to seek a home on earth outside of Jewry. The messianic community was to become in fact what it was in nature—the community of the world.

Philip the Hellenist went to Samaria and preached Christ there' (Acts 8:4-6). It was a likely place of refuge, for the Samaritans shared the Hellenist opposition to the Jerusalem Temple (Jn. 4:20). Other Hellenist Jews went to Antioch where for the first time they extended their apostolate to full-blooded Greeks (Acts 11:19f.). This new move away from Jewry served to emphasize the stress which had been present from the beginning. Christ was all in all for the new community: "They preached the Lord Jesus" (Acts 11:20). People sensed the emphasis. They took from it their cue in giving a name to this new group which had arisen in their midst. If Jesus were the Christ, the Messiah, they were Christians, the messianic community. "It was in Antioch that the disciples were first called 'Christians'" (Acts 11:26).

The Church of Christ was expanding. For "church of Christ" it truly was. Israel of old was called the *Qahal* (Septuagint—*ekklesia*) because it was the assembly of God's chosen people. For the same reason the new Israel was also the Church of God (*ekklesia tou theou*) and even more the Church of Christ, for He was its very life.

As it expanded this Church remained true to itself, taking direction from its leaders, drawing life from its word and sacrament. The story of Philip in Samaria is typical. "He went down to the city of Samaria and preached the Christ to them. . . . And when they believed Philip as he preached the kingdom of God and the name of Jesus Christ, they were baptized, both men and women" (Acts 8:5, 12). The preaching of the word and the acceptance of the sacrament are both essential in the life of the new community.

Quite as important, however, is the seal of approval from the only ones who could give approval and a full share in the riches of the community's life: "Now when the apostles in Jerusalem heard that Samaria had received the word of God, they sent to them Peter and John. . . . Then they laid their hands on them and they received the Holy Spirit" (Acts 8:14, 17).

It is noteworthy how large Peter looms in this whole picture of expanding Christianity as Luke presents it in Acts. He seems to move always in first place as spokesman and representative of the community (*cf.* Acts 1:55ff; 2:14-36; 3:1-11; 4:8ff; 5:3-11; *etc.*). There is, however, no blatant note in his claim to authority. He lives and works in a family where everyone knows and loves everyone else. In such surroundings he could fulfill perfectly the behest of Jesus that he who is first should be as he who serves: "Now when the apostles in Jerusalem heard that Samaria had received the word of God, they sent to them Peter and John" (Acts 8:14).

The new Israel threatened the old; the Christ-Lord of Christianity introduced a discordant note into the *Shema's* profession of faith: "Hear, O Israel! The Lord is our God, the Lord alone!" (Deut. 6:4). The soul of Paul, therefore, seethed with bitterness and the eradication of the Church became the burning passion of his life. He would stamp out this blasphemy; if need be, he would drown it in the blood of his fellow-Jews.

All this, however, was only the darkness before dawn. On the way to Damascus sunlight burst upon him in a blaze of glory and he heard the stunning words, "Saul,

Saul, why dost thou persecute me?" (Acts 9:4). In the twinkling of an eye Paul the hater of Christ became a Christian. The persecutor of the Church became its theologian.

Scholars like Lucien Cerfaux and Alfred Wikenhauser have written long, penetrating analyses of Paul's doctrine on the Church. It would be endless to rehearse their meticulous erudition. We desire, instead, to center attention on Paul's contribution not as a theologian but as a witness. When he entered the Church, it was already in existence and fully self-conscious. In his epistles, therefore, we touch the flesh and blood Church of the first-generation Christians. These earliest writings of the apostolic period bear glowing testimony to the life of the Church just as Paul found it, just as he knew it must remain.

There is no doubt that this man was a rugged individualist, the keen-sighted theologian of the early Church. In his epistles to the Galatians he is at his unique best, boasting flagrantly that his are the penetrating insights and the God-given message of liberty. The other Apostles seem merely to plod along in a pedestrian way: "What they once were matters not to me—God accepts not the person of man" (Gal. 2:6). Indeed, "When Cephas came to Antioch, I withstood him to his face, because he was deserving of blame" (Gal. 2:11). Restricting their view to texts like these, Baur and Strauss created the image of a Paul who opposes his gospel to the limited teaching of Peter and the Jewish element in the early Church.

Long ago, however, the Tübingen view of Paul has been discounted as myopic. It was based on Galatians and overlooked the other epistles. And even in Galatians it read only chapter 2 and conveniently forgot that there was also chapter 1.

There is no doubt that Paul was always conscious of his God-given authority; he is "an apostle sent not from men nor by man but by Jesus Christ and God the Father" (Gal. 1:1). This confidence rings in the salutation of all his letters. In making this claim, however, Paul has only one purpose—to validate his right to preach the Gospel of Christ.

He considered it his first duty to deliver to others the kerygma which had been in the Church from the beginning. Like all the Apostles he presented everywhere the saving truths which Matthew had jotted down in Aramaic as an official record of Peter's preaching in Jerusalem (*cf.* 2 Tim. 2:8). Paul could say to all his converts what he wrote to the Corinthians: "I delivered to you first of all what I myself received" (1 Cor. 15:3).

He knew well that every preacher would try to present the Church's teaching in the most attractive and compelling way he could. Paul himself theologized to his heart's content. He used the juridical and cultic thought-patterns of Jewry; he gave full rein to his knowledge of Stoic diatribe and utilized its antithesis in presenting the Christian message. He insisted, however, that these elucidations were valid only insofar as they presented the authentic Christian message. The preacher might build with gold, silver, precious stones, wood, hay, straw; but the essential factor consisted always in the foundation of the Church's saving message (*cf.* 1 Cor. 3:11f.).

This teaching of the Church must be safeguarded at any cost. When men showed too much concern with human philosophizing Paul went out of his way to center attention on the fundamental teaching itself. The Corinthians loved a display of "wisdom"; they listened delightedly to the brilliant phrases of Apollo and to his finely spun Alex-

andrian allegories. Paul sensed danger. Men might come
to prefer the tangible beauty of human words to the ineffable power of God's deeds. Paul, therefore, deliberately
avoided the brilliance of "wisdom" to present the simple
truths which Peter and James and John had recounted on
the morrow of Pentecost: "And I, brethren when I came
to you, did not come with pretentious speech or wisdom,
announcing unto you the witness of Christ. For I determined not to know anything among you, except Jesus
Christ and him crucified" (1 Cor. 2:1f.).

In every epistle Paul shows his reliance on the traditional teaching which is everywhere the same. Writing to
people like the Romans and Colossians, whom he has
never seen, the Apostle takes it for granted that they are
thoroughly familiar with the truths which he himself is
preaching. How often he bases his own doctrinal developments on this presumed knowledge: "Do you not know?"
"Have you not heard?" "Do you not remember?" Writing
to the Romans Paul takes it for granted that their primitive
credal formulary (Rom. 1:3f.) contains the same faith
which he himself would express with greater theological
exactness (*cf*. Rom. 9:5; Phil. 2:5-11). Writing to the
Colossians, who had been evangelized not by himself but
by Epaphras, he simply presumes that they know the
Church teaching from which he himself draws the contents
of his instructions (*cf*. Col. 1:5-7; 2:6f.).

This reliance on the traditional teaching made Paul suspicious of new customs (*cf*. 1 Cor. 11:16) and intransigently hostile to distortions of the primitive Gospel. He
was speaking of false teachers when he wrote: "If anyone
destroys the temple of God, him will God destroy; for
holy is the temple of God, and this temple you are" (1 Cor.
3:17).

This witness to the unchanging teaching of the Church is the first factor one must reckon with if one wishes to share Paul's mind on the Church. He who is looked upon as the most creative of the Apostles, the artisan of Christian theology, places his chief glory in being "approved by God to be entrusted with the gospel" (1 Thess. 2:4). In the traditional teaching which is always and everywhere the same Paul sees a dynamic power to save (Rom. 1:16f.). Through the Church message the risen Christ was able to enter the heart of every man to save and to sanctify.

Paul, therefore, could write to the Thessalonians in the first letter of his long correspondence: "We give thanks to God without ceasing, because when you heard and received from us the word of God, you welcomed it not as the word of men but, as it truly is, the word of God, which works in you who have believed" (1 Thess. 2:13). So long as the message was presented accurately and integrally Christ could do His work. When, therefore, the imprisoned Paul learned that others were busy preaching the Gospel in order to curry favor with the new converts, he cried out, "What of it? Provided only that in every way, whether for sincere or insincere motives, Christ is being proclaimed; in this I rejoice, yes, and I shall rejoice" (Phil. 1:18).

His mind is crystal clear. Christian life comes from a Gospel message which is fixed and credal and dynamically powerful. For Paul faith is not the fideism of blind surrender to an unknown God as it would be in the systems of Rudolph Bultmann and Paul Tillich. Paul's faith, instead, is dependent on the spoken word and reaches God truly through surrender to its conceptual element. For the Gospel is a mirror held up to the heart of God that it may reflect His thoughts into the heart of man (*cf.* 2 Cor. 3:18). As an Apostle, therefore, Paul considered it his prime duty to witness and to transmit, not to create: "Let a man so account us, as servants of Christ and stewards of the Mysteries of God. Now here it is required in stewards that a man be found trustworthy" (1 Cor. 4:1f.).

The Apostle's concept of sacramentality is a second factor which one must keep in mind in order to share his understanding of the Church. Scholars of the Lausanne school have suggested that for Paul salvation consisted in a mere psychological assent to the salvific deed of Calvary proclaimed by the Gospel. In that event God's intervention at Calvary would have no greater efficacy than His divine intervention on Sinai; and once more man would be left to himself and to his own devices.

Paul's teaching, on the other hand, presupposes that the believer is really and effectively united to the risen Christ as one body-person to another (*soma* to *soma*) in the sacramental rites of Baptism and the Eucharist. For Paul, Christ did not speak in a metaphor when, on the way to Damascus, He complained, "Saul, Saul, why are you persecuting me?"

The first time that Paul clearly asserts the realism of sacramental life in the Church is when he chooses to challenge an ugly problem on the level of its own realism. Christians of Corinth had fallen back into fornication, into commingling of body with body not merely as a physical experience but as a full personal interchange of thought and affection. Paul opposes the sin by appealing to another bond which the Christian has already contracted, the well-known bond between his person and the person of the glorified Christ which is as real as the union between a man and a harlot: "Do you not know that your bodies are members of Christ? Shall I then take the members of Christ and make them members of a harlot?" (1 Cor. 6:15).

In both cases the full person is involved in a real way. For Paul the Hebrew the word "body" does not have the same meaning as in our twentieth century Western vocabulary. Instead of denoting the physical part of the body-soul composite (as with us), the word "body" in Paul's vocabulary signifies the whole reality of man as an animated and personalized body living a fully human life. When, therefore, he speaks of the Christian's union with Christ his thought is very realistic. He sees all Christians as completing and extending one and the same person and life, Christ Himself.

This first allusion to the body of Christ is incidental to the main point of the passage where it is found. Yet it has a validity all its own because it expresses so aptly the realism of the Christian's union with Christ as Paul sees it and as he, or his disciple, will express it later in the consummate synthesis of his thought in Ephesians 5:25-32 where he likens the union of Christ and His Church to the bond between a devoted husband and wife. No union could be more intimate, because no dependence could be more complete. All that the Christian has as a Christian he receives in the total surrender of his body-person to the body-person of Christ: "You are in Christ Jesus, who has become for us God-given wisdom, and justice, and sanctification, and redemption (1 Cor. 1:30f.).

This union begins at Baptism, as Paul indicates in Galatians 3:27f. Though shifting his thought-pattern he maintains the dynamic realism of the Christian experience: "All you who have been baptized into Christ have put on Christ." The analogy is drawn from the action of putting on a garment; but, as G. Duncan points out in his commentary on Galatians: "In Scripture it denotes that the wearer becomes in a subtle way identified with what he puts on." The present text shows how intimate is the identification it evokes. For Paul goes on to affirm that in the psychosomatic rite of Baptism the body-person (*soma*) of the Christian is so totally surrendered to Christ that whatever is merely "flesh" disappears, so that "There is neither Jew nor Greek; there is neither slave nor free-man; there is neither male nor female. For you are all one person in Christ Jesus."

Paul, therefore, teaches clearly that Christian life involves a real and personal union between the individual Christian and the glorified Christ, a union in which the Christian depends so completely upon Christ that He alone functions as the directive spiritual force: "He who cleaves to the Lord is one spirit with him" (1 Cor. 6:17).

This same realism prevails when Paul comes to speak of Christians as a collectivity in his discussion of the Eucharist. Once more the point of departure for his memorable statement is a particular problem, the danger of syncretism arising from sharing in the banquets of pagan worship. The Apostle declares that such conduct is incompatible with the celebration of the Christian supper which joins the Christian to Christ: "The bread that we break, is it not the partaking of the body of the Lord?" (1 Cor. 10:16).

As proof of the real presence of Christ in the Eucharist Paul appeals to a fact which carried a barbed thrust to the disunited Corinthians. He recalls the truth which was recognized from the beginning; the remarkable fellowship (*koinonia*) of Christians with one another has its total cause in the fellowship (*koinonia*) of each individual with Christ in the breaking of the bread: "Because the bread is one, we though many are one body, we who partake of the one bread" (1 Cor. 10:17). In this text the "one body" is still the individual body-person of the risen Christ. The many are one body because the "one bread" makes each one concorporeal with Christ.

In the realism of Paul's thought, both Baptism and the Eucharist enable Christ to become "all in all," the one source and the only center of Christian life. Dr. Rawlinson, therefore, is on firm ground when he emphasizes the importance of the Eucharist as a prime element in shaping Paul's doctrine on the Church as the body of Christ.

For Paul, then, the Church was not merely a society founded by Christ to endure forever as the best way of saving men. It was far more the enduring sacrament of Christ's abiding presence among men, the real and permanent means He has chosen to fulfill His promise, "Behold, I am with you all days, even unto the consummation of the world (Mt. 28:20).

The Apostle constantly witnesses to this reality and permanence of Christ's presence in and through the Church. He likens the Church to a temple where God dwells and where His Son gives Him ceaseless praise (*cf.* 1 Cor. 3:16f.; 2 Cor. 6:16). He affirms that Christ cherishes the Church just as a devoted husband loves and cherishes his wife (Eph. 5:28-22). He is most expressive, however, when he speaks of the Church as the "body of Christ" (*cf.* 1 Cor. 12:12-27; Rom. 12:4f.; Col. 1:24; 2:19; *etc.*).

For Paul, Christ is "all in all." Whether he speaks of the individual Christian, the local congregation, or the whole Church, Paul sees all as belonging to the body of Christ, as completing and extending the person and life of the risen Christ Himself. For the Savior living gloriously in heaven is Himself the Body-Person, the one central figure with whom all Christians are intimately united and on whom they totally depend. In Paul's classic phrase they are "in Christ Jesus," precisely because He is in them as the total source of all spiritual life in the Church. "Here [in the Church] there is not 'Gentile and Jew,' 'circumcised and uncircumcised,' 'barbarian and Scythian,' 'slave and freeman'; but Christ is all things and in all." (Col. 3:11)

The Apostle's doctrine on the Church as the body of Christ gives special force to his teaching on authority. It is difficult to understand why Anders Nygren has spoken only of Paul's doctrine on the word and on the sacrament in his excellent monograph, *Christ and His Church*. The truth is that from the very beginning of his epistolary correspondence Paul shows a vital awareness of the function of authority in the Church.

He glories in his apostleship and boasts of his power because he knows well that the apostle is a *shaliah*—one sent by Christ with the fullness of His authority: "On behalf of Christ, therefore, we are acting as ambassadors, God, as it were, making appeal through us" (2 Cor. 5:20). This consciousness of bearing the authority of Christ was with Paul always and everywhere. He acted with complete liberty and aplomb whether he enjoined commands on those who were present or leveled threats against those who were absent. This confidence never failed him for he looked on himself always as the representative of Christ: "I have already warned, when present, and now in my absence I warn again . . . I will not spare. Do you seek a proof of the Christ who speaks in me, who is not weak in your regard, nay, is powerful in you? . . . We shall live with him through the power of God in your regard" (2 Cor. 13:2-4).

Paul recognized this same authority in other leaders of the Church. For it is clear in his epistles that others ruled the local churches during the absence of their father and founder. As in Judaism itself, elders (*presbyteroi*) were chosen to direct the conduct of the community. Besides this group—and probably selected from among them—

certain administrators (*episcopoi*) were empowered to watch over the needs of the community and to preside at its liturgical assemblies. From the very beginning Paul enjoined obedience to these men of authority (*cf.* 1 Thess. 5:12f.). The fact that they discharged their duties in the Church, the body of Christ, made the exercise of their authority a function of Christ Himself (*cf.* 1 Cor. 12:27f.; Rom. 12:4, 8).

As time went on, Paul would share more and more of his own power with subordinate officers, men like Titus and Timothy. What belonged to the Apostles eminently, the unique power of theirs which shaded all lesser authority, became more and more the possession of the local overseers. Yet even in the period of the pastoral epistles the local authorities had not yet received the full power of the monarchical bishop as present in St. Ignatius' letters. This transfer would become necessary only when death brought an end to Paul's over-all regency.

There is also, of course, the crucial question of Peter's authority. What did Paul think of it? He never answered this question, simply because he wrote out of a living tradition where Peter's role was taken for granted. His casual remarks, however, shed an aura of light about Peter as someone special in the ruling body of the Church.

After his conversion Paul paid a courtesy visit to Jerusalem to see Peter (*cf.* Gal. 1:18). Later in his apostolate at Antioch he was greatly disturbed when Cephas, of all people, placed a principle in jeoardy by discrimination against the Gentiles (*cf.* Gal. 2:11-14). At Corinth Paul had to accept the fact that one of the dissenting groups centered its loyalty on Peter, as though he had as much right to that loyalty as Paul and Apollo, the founders of the Corinthian Church (*cf.* 1 Cor. 1:12). For Paul as for the others Peter stands in a category of his own: "Have we not the right to take about with us a woman, as do the other apostles, and the brethren of the Lord, and Cephas?" (1 Cor. 9:15; *cf.* 15:5).

Paul's letters, therefore, reflect authentically what the rest of the Church thought about Peter. If he has left no formal proof of Peter's authority it is because, as Père Benoit has pointed out, this truth was a universally accepted part of the Church's life.

This long discussion of Paul's witness to the existence and nature of the Church finds its warrant in the uniqueness of his testimony. First, his epistles stand as the earliest extant record of everyday life in the Christian community (between 50 and 67 A.D.). Secondly, they come from a man who first knew Christianity as an unbeliever and a persecutor and who forfeited many privileges to accept its claim (*cf.* Phil. 3:3-8). Thirdly, the Church life he describes was being lived in persecuted communities which, like Paul himself, would have had everything to gain by reverting to earlier Judaic loyalties. Fourthly, Paul's value as a witness is all the more significant since it is so easy to distinguish it from his role as an original and creative thinker. His testimony, therefore, is not only a faithful transcript of life and practice in the Church but also a guarantee of its historical claim. A man of Paul's character and background would have been the last one in the world to "create" Christianity.

Other apostolic writings come from a later period; but their witness to the constituent elements of Church life matches the pattern of Paul's testimony. The Johannine writings, for example, though coming from the traditions of Asia Minor, are in perfect agreement with Paul's portrait of the Church. In them we find the same tenacious emphasis on the unchanging word (*cf.* 1 Jn. 1:3; 2:27; 2 Jn. 8:11) and on the true authority of those who watch over the Church: "He who knows God listens to us; he who is not of God does not listen to us" (1 Jn. 4:6). The whole Johannine Gospel is a witness to the sacramental sources of the Church's life.

Another independent witness may be found in the Greek Gospel of Matthew. Coming from the latter part of the first century, the distinctive mark of this Gospel is its delineation of the Church. It emphasizes the role and authority of the Petrine office (even at a time when Peter was himself already dead—(Mt. 16:17-20), the power of the Church leaders (Mt. 18:15-18), the presence of Christ in the liturgical assembly (Mt. 18:19f.), the unchanging firmness of the Church's word (Mt. 7:24-27). Moreover, as David M. Stanley writes, "by transposing a saying of Jesus regarding the Mystery of the Kingdom (*cf.* Mk. 4:11), Matthew shows the awareness that the Church in his day already possessed a body of doctrines which had been entrusted to the apostolic magisterium: 'to you the knowledge of the mysteries of the heavenly Kingdom has been confided' " (13:11).

Acts, Paul, John, Matthew—all the apostolic writings witness to the Word, the sacrament, and authority as constituent elements in the life of the Church. What connection does it all have with the Jesus of history? Some find it difficult to read the thought of the Church back into the mind of Jesus; the really impossible thing is to read it out of His mind. For if the Church did not come from Jesus, we are faced with the anomaly of an effect without a cause.

It is true that all that we know of Jesus comes from the Church of the first century, from writers who already believed in Him as the Risen Savior and the messianic Son of God. These records and memories, however, come from men who not only believed in Him as the Risen Savior and the messianic Son of God, but from disciples who had also lived with Him. They were well qualified to judge whether the kerygma of the Apostles misrepresented the facts of history. If, therefore, they became members of the Church and accepted its teaching and sacraments and leaders, it is only because they were convinced that the structure of the Church rested foursquare on the foundation which the Apostles affirmed was of Jesus' own making.

During His lifetime He had presented Himself in the role of Daniel's Son of Man (Dan. 7) and of Isaia's Suffering Servant (Is. 53). He was, therefore—in the light of this composite picture—a corporate personality, a Son of Man who embodies the "saints of God" (*cf.* Dan. 7:13f. with Dan. 7:25-27), a Suffering Servant who gives His life "for the many" (Is. 53:11f.). His death and glorification involved all; His fate would have weighty meaning in the lives of others. In the days of His earthly life, therefore, He took care to provide for the world-family which would come into being through the power of His resurrection.

If He had not actually made such preparations, the Jews of Jerusalem (who were eyewitnesses of His life) would have been the first to reject the Apostles' false claims. They had everything to lose and nothing to gain in accepting a merely fabricated Pentecostal message. This first generation of Jewish Christians, therefore, offers an irrefutable argument for the intimate bond between the Church of Pentecost and the Jesus of history.

It is only His choice and preparation that can explain why these first Christians turned from the learned doctors of the Law whom they had always venerated, to accept the religious leadership of ignorant Galilean fishermen whose very background disqualified them from all doctrinal or religious authority.

It is only the teaching of Jesus, illumined and corroborated by His resurrection, that can explain why men accepted a Word which not only altered the cardinal tenet of the *Shemá* ("Hear, O Israel! The Lord is our God, the Lord alone!"), but also cut through the maze of respected rabbinical doctrine to deep underlying principles which only the Creator of the Law could lay bare.

It is only the institution of Jesus that can explain why Jews who gloried in circumcision could come to restrict salvation to a rite which resembled the Baptism previously required only of heathen converts to Judaism. It is also only an act of Jesus that can explain why these same Jews chose the Christian "breaking of bread" as their true and only Passover celebration.

In His lifetime, therefore, Jesus prepared for the future life of His Church by choosing its leaders, by providing it with sacraments, and by ministering the Word which would form the heart of its teaching. Were this not so, the image of the primitive Church which looms so large and clear in the apostolic writings would remain forever an inexplicable anomaly.

CHAPTER 10 MARY,
PROTOTYPE
OF THE CHURCH

St. Paul spoke only once of the woman who gave birth to Christ (Gal. 4:4). He spoke numerous times of that other woman—the Church—who gives birth to Christ in us. It was on the road to Damascus that Saul, the persecutor, first confronted the blinding splendor of Christ in the Church. The scene is reminiscent of Moses' first contact with God on Sinai: lightning flashed and thunder roared, and a voice whispered eternal truth in a single word, "Saul, Saul, why dost thou persecute me?" (Act 9:4).

Years passed before Paul the Apostle understood fully all that these words contained—years of solitude in Arabia, years of suffering and preaching, years of conflict with error. But these were enriching experiences, for they won Paul a clear insight into the mystery of Christ. He saw "the Church in all her glory, not having spot or wrinkle or any such thing" (Eph. 5:27). Thereafter he could boast of total understanding: "You can perceive how well versed I am in the mystery of Christ" (Eph. 3:4). For he had come to know the Church with the full flush of personal discovery, so that in his letter to the Ephesians he speaks as though his knowledge of the Church is a new contribution to the deposit of faith.

In a way it was; for his glowing words have enlightened all men on "the mystery which has been hidden from eternity in God" (Eph. 3:9)—the mystery of Christ living in us, praying and working in us, sharing with us His riches. The fact is, however, that God Himself had previously intimated this wondrous plan. Every prophet of the Old Law had spoken of a searing purification to come and of "a third part," the remnant, which would emerge. These would be "the poor ones" of the new Israel, its *anawim* (Soph. 3:12-17; Zach: 13:8f.). Deutero-Isaia hails them as "the long-lived seed" of the Suffering Servant, children born of His agency to share His triumph (Is. 53:1). Ezechiel described them as little lambs tended lovingly by the Good Shepherd who claims them as His own (Ez. 34:10-16). All the words of the later prophets pulse with hope in the bright future of this chosen group who will cluster round their Redeemer to receive from Him the riches of redemption. The later psalms throb with the peace and triumph thrilling in their souls. Truly all the saints and sages of the postexilic period lived in constant vigil, awaiting expectantly the blessed day when at long last the Messiah and His "poor ones" would reap the harvest of victory.

Christ fulfilled this Old Testament hope. The first act of His redemptive work was to single out the greatest of the *anawim* and to dower her in the first moment of her conception with all His riches. No wonder this poor maid of Israel cried out, "My soul magnifies the Lord . . . because He has regarded the lowliness of His handmaid" (Luke 1:46, 48). She was the first to taste the fruit of Christ's victory.

But not the only one. The Divine Giant ran His course that He might share the glory of His triumph with all "the poor and needy" who formed His Church. He proclaimed this in the first sermon of His public life; for in the beatitudes He promised the redeemed of all time a full share in His riches. Summing up the virtues of the Old Testament *anawim* and gazing on His mother as their perfect type and pattern, He cried out, "Blessed are the poor in spirit, for theirs is the kingdom of heaven. Blessed are the meek . . . blessed are the clean of heart . . . blessed, indeed, are all 'the poor and needy' of the new Israel" (*cf.* Mt. 5:3ff.). He fulfilled this pledge on the first Pentecost when all His "poor and needy" disciples gathered in the upper room to receive the outpouring of His Spirit. And Mary was there in the midst of the charter members of the Church born on Good Friday, first and greatest of all, yet truly one of them.

This wonder of the *anawim* of the new Israel sharing fully in the riches of Christ is the mystery of the Church. St. Paul pondered it, preached it, lived it, until at last in his twin letters to the Ephesians and Colossians he gave it final and mature expression. From all eternity, he tells us, God planned to enclose all men in the sonship of His Divine Word and thus to bestow on them the graces of divine life. In Christ and through Him, every member of the Church bears a family resemblance to Him in the eyes of the Eternal Father; for "He predestined us to be adopted as His sons through Jesus Christ" (Eph. 1:5). Paul is enraptured by the grandeur of the divine plan. In his Epistle to the Ephesians he pours out his thought in floods of awesome praise that overflow the limits of sentence structure. He is forced to coin words since no superlative is strong enough to bear the weight of "the unfathomable riches of Christ" (Eph. 3:8). Indeed the unique style of this epistle, its grandiose periods and its crescendos of soaring enthusiasm, can be explained only by the exaltation that thrilled Paul's spirit as he contemplated the mystery of Christ's life in the Church.

This single theme of God's wondrous plan dominates all the Marian thoughts of the early Fathers. In our own decade scholars like Reindl, Arnold, Rahner, and Semmelroth have combed the patristic literature of the first four centuries to harvest the first-fruits of Marian theology. Perhaps the most complete and careful study is a work by Abbé Müller, *Ecclesia—Maria: Die Einheit Marias und der Kirche.* Out of these investigations has come an insight exceedingly rich in itself, though somewhat unfamiliar to the devotional thought of our own day. These scholars are agreed that the Fathers of the first four centuries do not highlight the aspects of Marian theology that shine gloriously under the searchlight of the "modern" investigation that began with Venerable Bede. Instead of concentrating on the uniqueness of Mary, these early Fathers present her simply as a member of the Church.

The key to their thought is the Pauline mystery of Christ, *i.e.,* the eternal plan of God that His Son incarnate should be the source of all that is good. In this perspective, Mary is the commencement of Christ's redemptive work in the world, the first and greatest member of the Church. Nowhere in the early Fathers, not even in St. Irenaeus, is she represented as the causal source of the Church's life. They associate her with Christ as the new Eve; but never do they speak of her as "mother of the living." Instead she is presented simply as the typical embodiment of what the rest of the Church should be. The teaching of Origen is characteristic. Like St. Paul, he describes the great wonder of Christianity as a rich mystical union between Christ, the Divine Word, and the Church. This union is accomplished in successive moments through the advent of the *Logos* into the world and into the lives of consecutive generations. The union of Christ with Mary, therefore, even though central and decisive, is still only one moment in the univocal process of union that dominates the whole life of the Church.

Thus it is the penetration of Christ's life into His Mystical Body that provides the dominant theme for the early Fathers. For them God's eternal plan is the paramount consideration; they see all things as energized by the mystery of Christ. The Church is the final term of this mystery and its perfect fulfillment, while Mary is simply its first and greatest member. Certainly these Fathers recognized a continuity between Mary and the rest of the Church. Thus, especially in the Eastern Fathers at the end of the fourth century, there is a marked fluidity, almost a "communication of idioms" of equivalence between Mary and the Church. However, in the Christocentric thought of the Fathers, the principle and cause of this continuity is not the spiritual energy of Mary influencing the Church, but the spiritual energy of Christ influencing both. For the writers of the first four centuries, Mary was always "the morning rising"—*quasi aurora valde rutilans.* For though dawn is joined to day, it does not cause the day. Rather it is the sun which illumines both. And so Mary was regarded simply as the first great work of the Sun of Justice, the perfect type of what He would do in a lesser way in all the *anawim* of the new Israel.

The mystery of Christ, therefore, is the key to early patristic teaching on the relation between Mary and the Church; it is also the clue to liturgical texts which breathe its spirit. For time and again the liturgy reflects this early attitude toward Mary. Instead of isolating her as a cause of the Church's riches, it often treats her simply as one of the Church's members. Thus in the Confiteor and in the Canon of the Mass her name is linked to those of Peter and Paul and the other saints as first among them in God's good favor, yet truly one of them. There is no indication of their dependence upon her; all are joined together as sharing Christ's power of intercession before the throne of the Father. Again, the liturgy often uses words which literally refer to someone other than Mary. Thus the previous Mass of the Assumption chose for its Gospel the story of the contemplative love of Mary of Bethany (Luke 10:38-42). To some this probably seemed incongruous, but not to those who understood the mystery of Christ. Both Mary the Mother of God and Mary of Bethany are members of the Church, who owe all that they have and are to the same Christ. What is said, therefore, of Mary of Bethany can be said with greater reason of Mary of Nazareth. Her rich share in the treasures of Christ is but the anticipation and type of all the graces of the whole Church.

To contemplate Mary in the light of the mystery of Christ does not obscure her pre-eminence. Though truly a member of the Church, Mary possesses in herself more grace than all others joined together. She is the masterwork of Christ, the full realization of all His plans for the Church. Thus the Church itself is already contained in the mystery of Mary, as its first actualization, its prototype and perfect exemplar. She contains eminently all that the Church should be; and so the Church must look to her and imitate her: *Sicut Maria, ita et Ecclesia*—what Mary is, the Church must be.

But even more than in her grace, Mary is the type of

the Church in her maternity. This, too, flows from the mystery of Christ. The whole plan of God began its fulfillment in the redemptive incarnation of the Divine Word in Mary; it achieves consummation in the new birth of this same Divine Word in the heart of every Christian. For it is only by uniting Himself to men that the Word accomplishes His mission. It was Mary's privilege to give Christ the physical life whereby He became Man; as St. Augustine has expressed it, her womb was the bridal chamber in which the Divine Word and humanity celebrated their nuptials. Through a maternity quite as real, the Church, "mother of all the living," must give Christ a mystical birth in the soul of every man, that every man can become Christian, united to Christ and sharing His riches. To each one she must repeat the words of St. Paul: "My dear children . . . I am in labor again, until Christ be formed in you!" (Gal. 4:19).

Thus the mystery of Mary's maternity is perpetuated and lives again in the maternity of the Church, Mother of Christ in each of His members. This is the most striking equivalence between Mary and the Church. They are both mothers of Christ: she pre-eminently as Mother of the physical Christ and the Church secondarily as Mother of the mystical Christ. Hence, between Mary and the Church there exists the same relation of identity as between the natural and the Mystical Body of Christ. That is why St. Clement of Alexandria, contemplating Mary, cries out, "And one alone, too, is the Virgin Mother. I like to call her the Church." And St. Leo, "It is by the same Holy Spirit that Christ is born of the all pure Virgin and that the Christian is born of the womb of the Holy Church." How often, too, this theme recurs in the liturgy. Every thought of Mary's motherhood, in the Masses of Advent and Christmastide, in the Marian anthems, prompts the earnest plea for a new birth of Christ in our own soul through the motherly action of the Church.

For what Mary has done as Mother, the Church herself must do—and in the same way. This is another feature of resemblance between the two mothers: both are virgins. They produce the same Christ, one in His physical nature, the other in His members, not through human device or carnal means, but through faith. The Divine Word, received by the faith of Mary and of the Church, is the only source of this maternity. Therefore, when a woman of the crowd praised Mary's physical maternity, our Lord Himself hastened to emphasize Mary's true cooperation through faith (Luke 11:28). How St. Augustine loved to return to this thought: *"Beata Maria, Quem credendo peperit, credendo concepit, prius mente quam ventre concipiens*—Blessed Mary begot in faith Him whom she conceived in faith, first conceiving in the spirit before she conceived in the womb."

It is in this virginal maternity of Mary, a virginity rendered fruitful by her faith, that the Church finds the perfect type and true model of the maternity which she must exercise day after day. Her solicitude in the liturgy for the purity of faith; her emphasis on the fruitfulness of those consecrated laborers who, though virgins, know a long-lived posterity through their work and prayer for the spread of the faith—all this gives eloquent expression to the Church's awareness that she must conform to Mary as type, model and pattern, if she would share in the fruitfulness of Mary's maternity.

It was left to later ages, however, to illumine the essential aspect of Mary's relation to the Church in the great mystery of Christ. In the 1951 Bulletin of the French

Society of Marian Studies, Père Barré, surveying Marian texts from the period of Venerable Bede to Albert the Great, emphasized the first appearance of our modern insight into our Lady's role. Whereas the early Fathers saw both Mary and the Church as successive moments in the unfolding of the mystery of Christ, the later Fathers sought deeper for the secret of Mary's pre-eminence. Today we bask in the light of their teaching. So great is Mary's share in the riches of Christ that she exerts a real causal influence on the rest of the Church. The ecclesiastical writers of the sixth to the twelfth centuries speak of her real cooperation with Christ in His divine work of redeeming the Church; they see her, as Mistress of the Apostles, mothering the infant Church; they celebrate her as Mother and Guardian of the whole Church.

At this period, then, the concept of Mary as the prototype of the Church gained a new richness. She was seen to be the model of the Church, not merely because she anticipated and surpassed the Church in her share of Christ's treasures, but even more because her very fullness is the means Christ uses to sanctify the Church. Hence, she is often spoken of as the *Caput Ecclesiae,* the head of the Church, subordinate to Christ who is the only true Head, yet truly sharing His authority over the other members of the Church. She is regarded also as the *Collum Ecclesiae,* the neck of the Church, since the grace of Christ the Head must pass through her if it is to reach his members. She is not merely a sister to the children of Christ in the Church; even more she is their mother. The grace-filling influence of her voice on the soul of John the Baptist, at the time of the Visitation, becomes the symbol of what she is always doing in the Church. Indeed, the very action of the Church in mothering souls not merely imitates Mary's divine maternity, but depends on the support of her motherly influence. Only through Mary does the Church become the Mother of Christ in souls. The whole pattern of the Church's life, all its goodness, its guidance, its defense, all that it has and all that it is — all depends upon her mediation.

It is this spiritual maternity that renders Mary the prototype par excellence of the Church. She is the perfect pattern of the Body of Christ because, as Pius XII said, she is "the most holy Mother of all His members." This theme enriches the greatest part of our liturgy. The Collects for all Mary's feasts, the very constituency of these feasts, the sequence *Stabat Mater,* and the Marian anthems that conclude the Divine Office — all these reflect the Church's awareness that Mary is truly the type of all her holiness and of all her actions, not merely as the first and greatest member of the Church, not merely as the first among those who share equally in the mystery of Christ, but above all else as the Mother who contains in herself eminently the very graces which the Church receives only through her mediation.

Such is the bond between Mary and the Church. Both are "the poor and needy" of the new Israel who owe all to their share in the mystery of Christ. Both have the same task of bringing Christ into the world. Yet the Church must always look up to Mary as utterly pre-eminent; it must model itself upon her as its prototype; it must honor her as a child honors its mother. For God could have spoken to the Church the words of Dante in the *Paradiso:* "Look now upon the face most like to Christ! For only its radiance can so fortify Thy gaze as fitteth for beholding Christ." And so, in obedience to God, the Church of every age must cry out to Mary with the fullness of complete dependence: Hail, Holy Queen, our life, our sweetness, our hope!

CHAPTER 11 THE SPIRIT
IN THE CHURCH
TODAY

C HRISTIAN life today is essentially what it has always been. Now as always man's striving for holiness is guided by the word of God and gains momentum through prayer and the sacraments. The apostolate, too, works for the end it has always pursued, to make the whole world one in Christ.

This sameness, however, is not monolithic. Something more than the passing of time differentiates the Church of 1963 from the Church of 1922. All living things adjust to the world around them. So, too, the Church. It shapes the dimensions of its service to the framework of the present time; it takes tone and color from its present surroundings.

Essentially the same yet perennially contemporary, the Church faces now as always the challenge of a contemporary world. If spiritual life is to be vital and the apostolate effective, men and women of the Church must keep their finger on the pulse of life around them.

The existentialism of Kierkegaard, Heidegger, and Sartre, as a philosophic system is on the wane. Its spirit, however, is still active. For one reason or another, people of our day are practical existentialists, keenly sensitive to the feel of experience in the here and now. The vast majority seem to live with nerve ends exposed to feel reality not through the wrappings of reflection but through the touch of experience.

Men of our time are intuitive, not reflective, with a sharp sense of what lies deep beneath the mere surface and beyond the facade. Feeling and realism: these are the focal points of contemporary thought and life. This is the *Zeitgeist* of the world around us, the spirit of both earthly men and spiritual men; no one escapes it.

This *Zeitgeist* is penetrating more and more into the spirit of the Church. Today our Catholic people are seeking true values and brook no substitute. Time-honored customs and long-standing traditions, man-made pedigrees and platitudinous clichés, vested interests and the practices of centuries are all being tested by fire. The burning heat of criticism dissolves the tinsel of pretense and the facade of make-believe. Nothing is too time-honored to escape the fire of passion for the real. Convention may still impose the attitudes of yesterday; it cannot shut the seeing eye or trammel the piercing mind.

This spirit can lead to unwarranted iconoclasm. The devouring flame of passion for the real can destroy not only the rind but the fruit, not only the shell but the meat which it encases. In Scripture studies scholars have had to save the Bible from the devastating fire of *Entmythologiezierung* —"demythologizing." Under the influence of the existential philosophy of Heidegger, men like Rudolph Bultmann and Karl Schmidt in Germany and F. C. Grant in our country have so demythologized the Gospels that they have left only the shadow of a merely human Jesus and the meaningless memory of a life without content or challenge.

The search for the real, on the other hand, if only it cherishes respect for what is truly real, truly unchanging, truly the teaching of Church, is bound to bring out what is richest in the Church's life. For the Holy Spirit is breathing in the *Zeitgeist* of our times, giving the power of His grace to our human search. It is His action as much as the spirit of the day which has forced our Catholics to measure up to tested standards of excellence. Facing squarely the compelling requirements of vital needs in our times, the Church in America has prepared a thoroughgoing plan for Sister formation and has launched signal advances in the fields of education, social work, and hospital administration.

The spiritual life of our people and the apostolic work of the Church are becoming more and more an expression of a passionate search for true and lasting benefits.

The spirit of our time is creating a new emphasis in the activities of the Church. Men seek nourishment no longer in crumbs which fall from the table but in the very food which God has provided in word and worship. At liturgical conventions it is obvious that our Catholic laity are seeking direct contact with the mystery of faith through enlightened participation in the sacred rites. They have also begun an intensive study of the Bible in CFM groups, Mr. and Mrs. Clubs, adult study-circles. In the spirit of our times Catholics are seeking the rich fullness of God's revelation.

The revision of our catechetical method is another evidence of this new interest. Men experience a malaise over previous patterns of religious instruction. Under the influence of the Eichstätt Conferences and of men like Hofinger, Goldbrunner, and Daniélou, under the impact of Lumen Vitae in Belgium, its ideals and methods, teachers of sacred doctrine in colleges and high schools, and leaders of Confraternity of Christian Doctrine work are driving for a new presentation of the faith.

They are convinced that the deepest reality of religion involves something more than the presentation of a speculative dogmatic system and a detached moral code. As the Redemptorist moralist, Father Häring, has pointed out, such systems lack full, dynamic realism until they are seen as part of the living encounter between man and God. A "Thou" and "I" dialogue must always figure as the authentic aim and sure guarantee of religious instruction. Our new catechisms will present the truths of the faith and the demands of morality in a kerygmatic framework. Everything will be integrated into the *Heilsgeschichte* of God's saving interventions in the world to claim from us an immediate loving response in the Body of Christ.

It is this same drive for the real which impels us to hew down walls of human making between men whom God would join together in one fold and under one shepherd. A few years ago Pope John XXIII did what no Pope before him would have dreamed of doing. For the moment he laid aside his office as Pontiff to speak as a man, as Joseph Roncalli. To a group of Jews who came to him, he spoke the greeting, "I am Joseph your brother."

In our country the spirit of seeking the real is tearing down walls between white and black; in the Church the same *Zeitgeist* is surging beyond the inaugural directives of the *Immortalium animos* of Pius XI to tear down walls of separation and to forge that real global unity which God has planned: "In Christ Jesus there is neither Jew nor Gentile, there is neither bond nor free . . . You are all one" (Gal. 3:28).

Diffident spirits are sometimes shocked by this passion for the real which burns in the hearts of many modern Catholics. Cardinal Alfrink's words at Strasbourg will stir opposition in men who are suspicious of the new spirit and who prefer to live in the secure mold and comfortable patterns of the past. On the other hand those who live vibrantly in the spirit of today will hear in the Cardinal's words a truth of deep, solid reality: "Could it not be that love for the Church and solicitude for non-Catholics should require, in our ecumenical era, that we sacrifice certain non-essential things? Could it not be that some things, no matter how dear to us and no matter how precious they might be for the Church, must be swept away because they obstruct a clear view of the Church?"

The heart of Cardinal Alfrink is alive with the spirit of the prophets of old. And to be a prophet is a glorious vocation. Its only requirement is that one have the light of God to see reality as He sees it and the courage to live by that vision.

Nothing in the life of the Church is escaping this process of being rethought and re-expressed. The old presentation of the virtues, the meaning of obedience, the concept of virginity, the relation between active and contemplative life, the sanctity of the laity — these thought-patterns are all being probed, not to discard them but to understand them truly and to see their full, rich role in man's encounter with God.

Even theological truth knows the same sifting. The work of Geiselmann and Tavard on the relation between Scripture and Tradition is typical. The new explanation of our Lord's action at the Last Supper proposed first by the non-Catholic Joachim Jeremias and developed by Père Benoit and Dom Dupont will greatly strengthen our presentation of the Eucharist as sacrifice. The work of Lyonnet and Dürrwell on the resurrection of Christ is bound to alter our concept of its role in the redemptive mystery.

Theologians like Karl Rahner, Yves Congar, Jean

Daniélou, Henri de Lubac, and in our country, John Court-
ney Murray and Gustav Weigel, Godfrey Diekmann and
George Tavard are men of our time, with a passionate zeal
to uncover what is deepest and richest in the Church's tradition. Dogmatic teaching is the frail human expression of
divinely revealed truth. Like everything human, its tone
and color and wording must be perfected if we are to con-
vey to others the Church's full understanding of what is
real in the heart of God's mystery.

This spirit is modern through and through; it is not
modernist. The contemporary theologian is a man of faith
who accepts all of God's revelation. Yet the very richness
of the revelation urges him to penetrate it ever more deeply
and to express it ever more exactly. He seeks to do what the
Church herself has done in perfecting at Chalcedon, at
Nicea, at Ephesus the human expression of the mystery of
Christ.

The modernist, on the other hand, is not a believer. He
recognizes nothing divine or revealed in the deposit of faith.
For him dogmatic truth is the projection of the human mind
authentically expressing its own inward drives. If a modernist alters previous teaching he does so in order to express
more clearly his interpretation of himself and to perfect
what is totally of human fabrication.

There are some, it is true, who will always suspect mod-
ernism in whatever is modern. Those who find comfort in
the customary will shout insubordination and doctrinal de-
viation, just as the priests of old shouted heresy before the
realism of Jeremia's preaching. But this cry is only the
gasp of a dying order. The living power of the wine of the
Spirit will burst the old wineskins.

Look around our country. The Sister formation movement is here to stay; liturgical participation is a force which
nothing will check. Go to any convention, the biblical, the

theological, the liturgical, the mariological, CFM, CCD; and you will see that the new wine is in ferment. More and more this spirit is coming into the seminaries, which means it is the spirit of tomorrow's priests. Look at the periodicals which are alive to what is best in the Church; *Theology Digest* provides a fair cross section. Here we find the thinking of theologians guided by the Spirit, the thought of an elite which will penetrate inevitably to the masses. Present unbelief stems partially, at least, from the unbelief of nineteenth-century intellectuals. What great minds are thinking today, the masses will be thinking tomorrow.

Fruitful Catholic life today as always requires man to hold fast to the Church, pillar of truth and source of all holiness. Our very *Zeitgeist* necessitates now, more than ever before, that all Catholics be solidly anchored in dutiful obedience to the Church, in dependence upon her teaching, in love for her institutions, her sacraments and her liturgy, in absolute respect for the magisterium.

This means very simply that men and women must become more and more Church-conscious. The full life of a Christian is found only in the Church which Christ founded to be the source of all life. If we close our eyes to the light of the Church, and shut off our concern from the interests of the Church, we shall grow tepid in holiness and become ineffective in the apostolate. All Catholics because they are Catholics, are committed to ecumenism, to the revival of liturgy, to the renewal of sacred studies, to the activation of the laity, to the mission-mindedness of the Church, to its yearning for peace, to its awareness of all life as sacramental.

The concerns of the Church must be our concerns; the advance of the Church must be our advance if we are to meet the challenge of our vocation as Christians.

This fruitful life with the Church involves at the same

time a dynamic life in the world. For the Church is in the world to meet it at every corner, to save it on every street, to sanctify it in every home. A Church which refuses to breathe the air of the world which God has created would not be the Church of Christ, for that Church must always live the words He prayed: "I do not pray that thou take them out of the world, but that thou keep them from evil" (Jn. 17:15).

To be authentically of the world, men of the Church must be ready to meet the world's tested standards. They must be as earnest in *seeking the real* as are the modern existentialists all around them and as competently vocal in expressing the true real.

No area of authentic human life can be "off-limits" for a truly integral Catholic. He is in the world to save it, not to fly from it. He above all others must plunge into the flood-stream of good which men of the world are trying to accomplish, identifying himself with those movements and personalities which are using what is humanly good to achieve what is humanly best.

Every area of human life, precisely because it is human, should be open to us. Politics or ballet, freelance writing or a roving State Department assignment, poetry or factory work: all this is our rightful domain, where Catholics must come to grips with reality, charge it with human goodness, and open it wide to the peace and blessing of God.

This is the challenge we face today. As men of our times we must seek what is real in all human values. As Catholics we must inspirit these real values with what is best in the Church.